SERIES EDITORS

TRACY L. PELLETT   **JACK RUTHERFORD**   **CLAUDIA BLACKMAN**

Skills, Drills & Strategies for
Tennis

Jack Rutherford

Holcomb Hathaway, Publishers
Scottsdale, Arizona 85250

Library of Congress Cataloging-in-Publication Data

Rutherford, Jack.
   Skills, drills & strategies for tennis / Jack Rutherford.
      p.   cm. — (The teach, coach, play series)
   Includes index.
   ISBN 1–890871–14–1
   1. Tennis.   I. Title.   II. Title: Skills, drills, and strategies for
tennis.   III. Series.
GV995.R828 1999
796.342—dc21   98–35650
                                             CIP

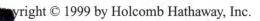
Holcomb Hathaway, Publishers, Inc.
6207 North Cattle Track Road
Scottsdale, Arizona 85250

10 9 8 7 6 5 4 3 2

ISBN 1-890871-14-1

Printed in the United States of America.

Contents

SECTION 4   Strategies   61

SECTION 5   Glossary   81

About the Author

Jack Rutherford is Director of the Seabury Wellness Center at Berea College in Berea, Kentucky. A former competitive player, Dr. Rutherford was elected to the Tennis Hall of Fame at his alma mater. He went on to coach and teach tennis at the college level and has worked with tennis players of all ages and abilities for the past twenty-five years. He received his doctorate in exercise and wellness education from Arizona State University and has been a prolific author with more than 100 professional articles and presentations on many health and physical education topics. Dr. Rutherford currently writes a popular newspaper column on wellness, has been recognized for his excellence as a teacher, and was Kentucky's Health Educator of the Year in 1997. He is widely sought after as a speaker on various topics.

Dr. Rutherford currently resides in Richmond, Kentucky, with his wife Pat and three children, Jasmine, Christopher, and Jeffrey. This book is dedicated to his father, Owen Rutherford, who taught him the game of tennis.

Preface

WELCOME TO THE *TEACH, COACH, PLAY* SERIES

The books in the *Teach, Coach, Play* series emphasize a systematic learning approach to sports and activities. Both visual and verbal information are presented so that you can easily understand the material and improve your performance.

Built-in learning aids help you master each skill in a step-by-step manner. Using the cues, summaries, skills, drills, and illustrations will help you build a solid foundation for safe and effective participation now and in the future.

This text is designed to illustrate correct techniques and demonstrate how to achieve optimal results. Take a few minutes to become familiar with the textbook's organization and features. Knowing what to expect and where to look for material will help you get the most out of the textbook, your practice time, and this course.

TO THE INSTRUCTOR

Your needs are changing, your courses are changing, your students are changing, and the demands from your administration are changing. By setting out to create a series of books that addresses many of these changes, we've created a series that:

- Provides complete, consistent coverage of each sport—the basics through skills and drills to game strategies so you can meet the needs of majors and non-majors alike.
- Includes teaching materials so that new and recently assigned instructors have the resources they need to teach the course.
- Allows you to cover exactly the sports and activities you want with the depth of coverage you want.

What's in the *Teach, Coach, Play* Series?

- Nine Activities:
    Skills, Drills, & Strategies for Badminton
    Skills, Drills, & Strategies for Basketball
    Skills, Drills, & Strategies for Bowling
    Skills, Drills, & Strategies for Golf

Skills, Drills, & Strategies for Racquetball
Skills, Drills, & Strategies for Strength Training
Skills, Drills, & Strategies for Swimming
Skills, Drills, & Strategies for Tennis
Skills, Drills, & Strategies for Volleyball

- Accompanying instructor's manuals

What's in the Student *Teach, Coach, Play* Textbooks?

The basic approach in all of the *Teach, Coach, Play* activity titles is to help students improve their skills and performance by building mastery from simple to complex levels.

The basic organization in each textbook is as follows:

Section 1 overviews history, organizations and publications, conditioning activities, safety, warm-up suggestions, and equipment.

Section 2 covers exercises or skills, participants, action involved, rules, facility or field, scoring, and etiquette.

Section 3 focuses on skills and drills or program design.

Section 4 addresses a broad range of strategies specifically designed to improve performance now and in the future.

Section 5 provides a convenient glossary of terms.

Supplements to Support You and Your Students

The *Teach, Coach, Play* books provide useful and practical instructional tools. Each activity is supported by its own manual. Each of these instructor's manuals includes classroom management notes, safety guidelines, teaching tips, ideas for inclusion of students with special needs, drills, lesson plans, evaluation notes, test bank, and a list of resources for you.

Preliminaries

History

From the finely manicured lawns of **Wimbledon,** England, to the red clay of **Roland Garros,** France, to the hardcourts of **Flushing Meadows,** New York, tennis is indeed an international game. Part of its worldwide appeal may have come from the game's rich and varied history. Tennis is thought to have been derived from a type of handball played by ancient Greeks and Romans who batted a ball back and forth with their hands. Once introduced to Europe, French ladies and noblemen stretched a rope across a room to serve as a net, and hit a ball back and forth, first with the open hand and later with an all-wood paddle. This earliest recognizable form of tennis was called "Le Jeu du Paume," or "the game of the palm." Tennis grew in popularity despite the fact that it was banned twice, first in the tenth century by Louis IV, who believed the game undignified, and later by Louis X in the fourteenth century, who maintained that tennis should be a "Sport for Kings only."

Tennis found its way to fourteenth-century England (perhaps because royal families of England and France often intermarried) where it became popular among the nobility. "Paume" experts came to England from France to promote the game's development. Eventually Paume was again outlawed because the King thought that time spent by soldiers playing tennis was taking away from their archery practice. It has been speculated that the game's name was probably derived around this time from the French word *tenez,* meaning "play" or "take it." Shouts of "tenez," heard during thirteenth- and fourteenth-century matches in France, were often reported back to England.

In England, the game developed slowly during the next two hundred years because of flagging interest, wagering on matches, and the banning of public play of Le Jeu du Paume during part of the seventeenth century. When Major Walter Wingfield introduced "lawn tennis" to England in 1873, the sport was being played only by the well-to-do. Wingfield's version of the game, played on grass, was known as "spharistike," after the Greek word for "ball," and consisted of a fifteen-point game in which only the server could score points. Spharistike was played on an hourglass-shaped **court** divided by a seven-foot-high net.

HISTORY, CURRENT STATUS, AND FUTURE OF THE GAME

Wimbledon
Roland Garros
Flushing Meadows

court

1

In 1874, while on vacation in Bermuda, Mary Outerbridge watched British soldiers playing spharistike using rackets shaped like snowshoes with strings. She brought rackets, ball, and a net back to the United States and is credited with establishing the first tennis court on U.S. soil, on the lawn, to be precise, of the Staten Island Cricket and Baseball Club. The sport was quickly embraced in the United States, developing into a competitive and skillful game.

The beginning tennis player is often perplexed by the game's unusual scoring system, the origins of which remain somewhat of a mystery to this day. The prevalent theory is that in early France, the most common silver piece was worth 60 sous, and its four parts 15 sous each. Tennis was played for stakes, so points were worth 15, 30, or 45 sous. Later, after the association with currency was dropped, 45 was shortened to 40 because it was easier to say. The term *love* is thought to have come from the French word *l'oeuf,* meaning "the egg" or "zero."

USTA

In 1881 the United States Lawn Tennis Association was founded and became America's governing body for the standardization of rules, equipment, and tournament play. Now called the United States Tennis Association, the **USTA** has spent considerable resources in promoting and developing tennis nationwide.

Tennis Today

Tennis's rich history has undoubtedly contributed greatly to its international appeal. In addition, the game's rules and scoring have been adopted worldwide; consequently, players and spectators from Canada to Japan to Romania share an understanding of the game when playing or watching.

ace

Although tennis was once played only by amateurs, players today often turn professional in their teens and retire from tournament play in their twenties. Few, however, give up the sport entirely. Tennis has many special qualities that keep players coming back again and again: the exhilaration of serving an **ace;** the challenge of struggling against a tough opponent; the internal battle with one's own emotions; the camaraderie that is shared by players after a match. For these and many other reasons, tennis is a game that players can enjoy for a lifetime.

The Future of Tennis

Many aspects of tennis have changed in recent years. Televised events such as Wimbledon and the U.S. Open have netted a larger following for the game, resulting in substantial increases in players, services, and products. Technological advances in rackets have resulted in larger head sizes and space-age materials such as graphite, boron, and ceramic. These advances have changed tennis to more of a power game. Public opinion polls have suggested that this may have reduced spectator interest at the professional level. Tennis governing bodies have been examining rules and equipment in an attempt to make the game more spectator-friendly. Using tennis **nap** balls with more **nap** to slow down the game has been one suggestion. The tennis enthusiast is undoubtedly interested to see what changes will be made in the future.

TENNIS ORGANIZATIONS

The United States Tennis Association (USTA)
51 E. 42nd Street
New York, NY 10017
(212) 949-9112

USTA Education and Research Committee
729 Alexander Road
Princeton, NJ 08540
(609) 452-2580

U.S. Professional Tennis Association (USPTA)
c/o Saddlebrook
P.O. Box 7077
Wesley Chapel (Tampa), FL 34249
(813) 973-3777

The Association of Tennis Professionals (ATP)
319 Country Club Road
Garland, TX 75040
(214) 494-5991

Women's Tennis Association (WTA)
1604 Union Street
San Francisco, CA 94123
(415) 441-1041

The International Tennis Federation (ITF)
Church Road, Wimbledon
London SW19 5TF
England

TENNIS PUBLICATIONS

International Tennis Weekly
Inside Women's Tennis
Journal of Physical Education, Recreation and Dance
Tennis Magazine
Tennis, USA Magazine
U.S.T.A. Yearbook
World Tennis Magazine

THE NATIONAL TENNIS RATING SYSTEM

The USTA has developed a self-rating system to help players determine their level of play for both recreational and tournament programs. Players using the rating system should assume they are playing someone of the same sex and ability.

1.0 This player is just starting to play tennis.

1.5 This player has limited playing experience and is still working primarily on getting the ball over the net; has some knowledge of scoring but is not familiar with basic positions and procedures for singles and doubles play.

2.0 This player may have had some lessons but needs on-court experience; has obvious stroke weaknesses but is beginning to feel comfortable with singles and doubles play.

2.5 This player has more dependable strokes and is learning to judge where the ball is going; has weak court coverage or is often caught out of position but is starting to keep the ball in play with other players of the same ability.

3.0 This player can place shots with moderate success; can sustain a rally of slow pace but is not comfortable with all strokes; lacks control when trying for power.

3.5 This player has achieved stroke dependability and direction on shots within reach, including forehand and backhand volleys but still lacks depth and variety; seldom double-faults and occasionally forces errors on the serve.

4.0 This player has dependable strokes on both forehand and backhand sides; has the ability to use a variety of shots including lobs, overheads, approach shots, and volleys; can place the first serve and force some errors; is seldom out of position in a doubles game.

4.5   This player has begun to master the use of power and spins; has sound footwork; can control depth of shots and is able to move opponent up and back; can hit first serves with power and accuracy and place the second serve; is able to rush net with some success on serve in singles as well as doubles.

5.0   This player has good shot anticipation; frequently has an outstanding shot or exceptional consistency around which a game may be structured; can regularly hit winners or force errors off of short balls; can successfully execute lobs, drop shots, half volleys, and overhead smashes; has good depth and spin on most second serves.

5.5   This player can execute all strokes offensively and defensively; can hit dependable shots under pressure; is able to analyze opponents' styles and can employ patterns of play to ensure the greatest possibility of winning points; can hit winners or force errors with both first and second serves. Return of serve can be an offensive weapon.

6.0   This player has mastered all of the above skills; has developed power and/or consistency as a major weapon; can vary strategies and styles of play in a competitive situation. This player typically has had intensive training for national competition at junior or collegiate levels.

6.5   This player has mastered all of the above skills and is an experienced tournament competitor who regularly travels for competition and whose income may be partially derived from prize winnings.

7.0   This is a world-class player.

CONDITIONING FOR TENNIS

Some players play tennis to get in shape. However, experts agree that conditioning that develops as a by-product of play is not likely to be sufficient to allow players to play up to their capabilities. Serious tennis players therefore need to increase their ability to perform maximally throughout a match by following a thorough conditioning program that focuses on the many fitness components needed.

baseliner

serve and volleyer

skill-related fitness

Because tennis varies considerably in intensity and duration, high levels of all physical and motor fitness components are important. The **baseliner** needs adequate cardiovascular and muscular endurance to sustain long baseline rallies. The **serve and volleyer** needs superior strength to execute powerful offensive shots. Flexibility is important when the player must stretch for a well-angled groundstroke. **Skill-related fitness** components such as agility, coordination, speed, balance, and reaction time are also needed to perform the game at a high level. The conditioning program described on the following pages emphasizes these fitness components in specific training routines.

Cardiovascular Endurance

Because tennis is an intermittent activity that features short to moderate bursts of energy followed by brief periods of rest, the anaerobic metabolic pathways are primarily used. Conditioning the tennis player's body to sustain effort in the presence of decreasing oxygen is, therefore, the most specific way to increase cardiovascular endurance. Two methods, interval training and fartlek training, are efficient methods of conditioning the anaerobic pathways for tennis.

Interval Training

interval training

Interval training is a formal conditioning system that consists of high-intensity running over prescribed distances with predetermined rest periods. A track or area

TABLE 1.1	Interval training program	
Week	**Total Distance**	**Work Intervals**
1	$1/2$ mile (880 yards)	1×440; 1×220; 2×110
2	$3/4$ mile (1320 yards)	2×440; 1×220; 2×110
3	1 mile (1760 yards)	2×440; 3×220; 2×110
4	$1 1/8$ miles (1980 yards)	1×660; 2×440; 4×110
5	$1 1/4$ miles (2200 yards)	1×660; 2×440; 3×220
6	$1 3/8$ miles (2420 yards)	2×440; 4×220; 6×110
7	$1 1/2$ miles (2640 yards)	2×660; 2×440; 2×220
8	$1 5/8$ miles (2860 yards)	2×660; 2×440; 3×220
9	$1 3/4$ miles (3080 yards)	2×660; 2×440; 4×220
10	$1 7/8$ miles (3300 yards)	2×660; 3×440; 3×220
11	2 miles (3520 yards)	2×660; 3×440; 4×220

with known distances is normally used. A stopwatch is needed to monitor the work intervals. Work intervals typically range from 110 to 440 yards, although longer work intervals such as 660 yards are not uncommon. As a general rule, the longer the work interval, the longer the corresponding active rest period. Rest intervals should be active; that is, slow jogging or brisk walking. For example, a 220-yard run should likely be followed by a 440-yard active rest period, twice the work interval. Active rest promotes faster recovery than sitting or lying down because the waste product of active work, lactic acid, needs to be removed from muscles through movement. Adequate recovery between interval training workouts is also important. Workouts performed every other day will promote faster development than daily routines. Some experts suggest that there be no more than two interval training workouts per week.

Following the seasonal plan in table 1.1 will result in weekly increases in the total distance run in interval training workouts. Warming up before the workout (light jogging), and cooling down (jogging and stretching) afterward should accompany this training program.

Fartlek Training

Fartlek training is a less formal but no less effective method of conditioning that can be used as an adjunct to or as a replacement for interval training. Fartlek training consists of high-speed bursts of running interspersed with slow jogging. Fartlek training is an excellent way for a beginner to develop the conditioning necessary to withstand the more rigorous demands of interval training. The advantage to this type of training is that no facilities (e.g., running track) or equipment (e.g., stopwatch) are needed.

The training variables in fartlek training—intensity, duration, and jogging/rest periods—may or may not be fixed as in interval training. As a general rule, one should follow a faster-paced run with a slow jog. Sprinting the distance between alternate lamp poles on a residential street is an example of fartlek training. The perceived exertion level of the activity is often used instead of a stopwatch to determine the intensity of training. Faster-paced runs should be at or near maximum

fartlek training

effort to improve the cardiovascular system. Slow jogging between the faster-paced runs serves as the active rest period, allowing the body time to recover. The beginner should start at roughly one-half to one mile of total running and work up from there. You will discover that you can progressively increase the pace runs because the body will adapt to the gradual overload placed upon it. The overall distance run from week to week should increase in a fartlek training program.

Weight Training

The importance of developing the tennis player's potential for muscle strength, endurance, power, and flexibility cannot be overstated. An overall weight-training program for the tennis player is likely to take between 45 and 60 minutes. Workouts should be spaced at least 48 hours apart to allow the muscle rebuilding process to adequately occur.

progressive resistance exercise (PRE)

Weight training, or **progressive resistance exercise (PRE),** consists of exercises for specific muscle groups, performed against designated resistance. A resistance or weight that can be lifted approximately 10 times should be selected for each exercise. Exercises should be repeated 8 to 12 times, or reps. This will ensure a balance between strength and muscular endurance development. The exercise should be done throughout the full range of joint motion using correct lifting technique. The down phase of the movement should take about twice as long to execute as the up phase. Beginners should initially perform one set of each exercise, progressing up to two and eventually three sets once the muscles have adapted to the total overload placed on them.

Players can modify any PRE training plan to fit their more specific needs. For example, if a player wanted to increase power, the resistance of the exercise should increase from 85 percent to 95 percent of maximum levels and the repetitions performed should decrease (3 to 5 reps). In addition, the upward movement should be executed as quickly as possible with proper technique.

The following exercises in table 1.2 are specifically designed to maximize the development needed by tennis players. For illustrative purposes, the Cybex strength system has been selected, although many others are available. Many experts still believe that conditioning with free weights more closely imitates the synergistic movements performed in tennis.

The PRE training program begins with the larger muscle groups and progresses to the smaller ones. Muscles that stabilize joints to allow more efficient movement are also included.

WARM-UP AND COOLDOWN

Warm-up

The tennis player who hits the ball without adequate warm-up courts disaster. Since muscles are packed in body fluid, it is well known that warm-up increases body temperature and blood flow to the area, reducing muscle viscosity. This reduces the chance of injury and improves performance.

The first phase of the warm-up should be general activity to increase the body's core temperature. Light jogging on the spot or around court lines, or jumping jacks for 3 to 5 minutes is usually adequate, although this may vary according to climate. Perspiration is usually a good sign of an increased core temperature.

The second phase of the warm-up involves stretching the specific muscles to be used. Static or slow stretching of muscles throughout their length (but not to the point of pain) is performed initially. Stretching 10 to 60 seconds for each muscle group elongates muscles and loosens the surrounding connective tissue, improving flexibility. See the box on the following page for suggested stretches.

Stretching Guidelines

Stretching can be more effective if some basic guidelines are followed:

1. It is best to stretch a muscle when it is in a relaxed state, not when it is contracted and/or weight bearing.

2. Never stretch with a jerking or bobbing motion.

3. Always stretch and hold in a static state for 15 to 30 seconds to allow the muscle to relax and stretch to its maximum.

4. Stretch the muscles controlling joints that will be used in the activity.

5. Some discomfort is not unusual during proper stretching. However, pain is a sign of a possible problem. Discontinue any stretch that causes pain. For tennis, the following stretches are suggested:

■ Shoulder #1

Extend the right arm up and across the body just under the chin. With the left hand, reach up and lightly pull the right elbow toward the left shoulder, keeping the right arm fully extended. Hold. Repeat with the left arm.

■ Shoulder #2

From a position slightly behind you, have a partner grasp your right wrist. Assume a forward stride position with the right foot forward. Slowly attempt to move your right arm forward while your partner resists slightly. Repeat with left arm.

■ Shoulder #3

Raise your arm and racket up and so that the racket is pressing slightly against the back of your head. Slowly move the arm forward, using the racket pressure against the head as resistance.

■ Neck

Keeping the shoulders stationary, turn the head repeatedly from left to right in a slow, rhythmic manner. Next, using the same manner, tilt the head to the right, then left several times. Finally, tilt the head forward slowly until the stretch is obtained. Never hyperextend the neck.

■ Trunk #1

From a standing position, with hands to the sides, push the right hand down the outside of the thigh as far as possible while raising the left shoulder. Keep both feet flat on the ground. Hold. Repeat on the left side.

■ Trunk #2

In a standing position, grasp the right wrist with the left hand. Slowly pull the right side of the body so that the trunk twists as far as possible. Repeat on the other side.

■ Trunk #3

From a standing position, establish a slight bend in the knees and bend forward at the waist. Roll the shoulders forward and hang both arms as far down as possible. This is not a hamstring stretch, so relax the legs. Also, relax the lower back, allowing the upper trunk to hang and stretch. Hang for at least 10–15 seconds.

■ Groin

In a standing position with feet shoulder-width apart, lean to one side, forcing the knee on that side to flex to almost 90 degrees. Repeat on the other side.

■ Legs

Standing, raise one leg and place on the top of the net (leave a slight knee bend). Lean forward and reach for the toes, relax the hamstrings, then hold. Repeat using other leg.

■ Calf/Achilles

Stand, facing the fence or net post, at a distance of about 3 feet. Step back about 12 more inches with the right foot. Lean forward with both arms extended to the fence/net post. Bend the left knee and straighten the right knee. Push the right heel to the court and lean the hips and upper body closer to the fence/net post. Relax the lower right leg muscles and hold. Repeat with the left leg.

■ Abdomen

In a standing position with the racket raised in one hand above the head, bend the upper body backwards as far as possible, stretching the abdominal muscles. Repeat with the other hand holding the racket above the head.

This is not a complete list of all the possible stretches that may be performed. However, these stretches do include each major muscle group involved in tennis. Add any other stretches preferred or necessary to feel prepared for participation in a vigorous game of tennis.

TABLE 1.2 Progressive resistance training	
MACHINE	**EXERCISE**
Legs	
Cybex Leg Press	Leg press
Cybex Leg Extension	Leg extension
Cybex Seated Leg Curl	Leg curl
Cybex Multihip	Leg abduction
Cybex Multihip	Leg adduction
Trunk/Back/Stomach	
Cybex Rotary Torso	Trunk rotation
Cybex Back Extension	Back extension
Cybex Lat Pulldown	Lat pulldown
Cybex Abdominal	Abdominal curl
Shoulders/Chest/Arms	
Cybex Shoulder Press	Seated press
Cybex Lateral Raise	Lateral raise
Cybex Shoulder	
Internal/External	Shoulder internal
Rotation	Rotation
Cybex Shoulder	
Internal/External	Shoulder external
Rotation	Rotation
Cybex Cable Column	Lateral raise
Cybex Cable Column	Shoulder flexion/adduction
Cybex Chest Press	Seated press
Cybex Arm Curl	Biceps curl
Cybex Tricep Press	Triceps curl
Cybex Wrist and Forearm	Flexors, extensors, pronators, supinators

The third phase of the warm-up should include sport-specific dynamic (game-like) movements that mirror the skills used in tennis. These exercises stretch the muscles to be used even further and should be done with the tennis racket in hand (or with the racket cover on the head of the racket for greater resistance). Speed of the movement should increase with each repetition until game speed is reached. These three phases of the warm-up should take approximately 10 to 15 minutes.

Following the warm-up exercises, players should pair up and begin hitting the ball back and forth across the net. For each shot, the pace should be slow at first, then increase gradually. Players should accentuate good stroke mechanics during warm-up to groove the strokes faster. The following sequence of tennis skill practice is typically used:

1. Groundstrokes (see figure 1.1).

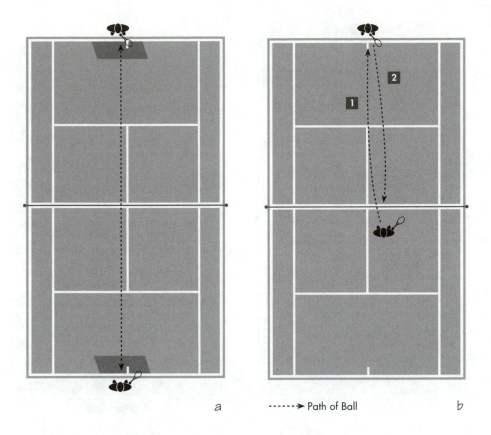

a   - - - - - ➤ Path of Ball   b

Figure 1.1
Groundstrokes
warm-up (a).

Figure 1.2
Volley warm-up (b).

2. One player at the net volleys, the other at the baseline hits groundstrokes, then players switch (see figure 1.2).

3. One player hits lobs while the other hits overheads, then players switch (see figure 1.3).

4. One player serves while the other player retrieves the serves (no return of serve), then players switch. Players should be sure to practice serving from right and left sides because no practice serves are allowed once the game begins. If not a formal match, return of service is generally permitted and should be a part of the warm-up routine (see figure 1.4).

The hitting phase of the warm-up should last at least 15 minutes so that both players have adequate time to practice all strokes. The beginning player typically hurries the warm-up to get to the game, whereas the veteran player carefully uses the allotted time to practice all strokes to be called upon in the game.

Cooldown

After a practice session, lesson, or match, it is just as important to cool the body down to a normal state as it is to warm up for the activity. Sudden stopping of vigorous physical activity puts a strain on the cardiovascular system. The cooldown also may help to reduce some of the muscle soreness typically associated with vigorous physical activity. Think of the cooldown as the reverse of the warm-up. Two phases are typically used:

1. Walk on or around the court area until you feel your heart rate slow to under 100 beats per minute. *(Sitting or lying down immediately after a match may cause light-headedness.)*

2. Repeat any of the static stretching exercises described in the warm-up.

Figure 1.3
Lobs and smashes
warm-up (a).

Figure 1.4
Serving warm-up (b).

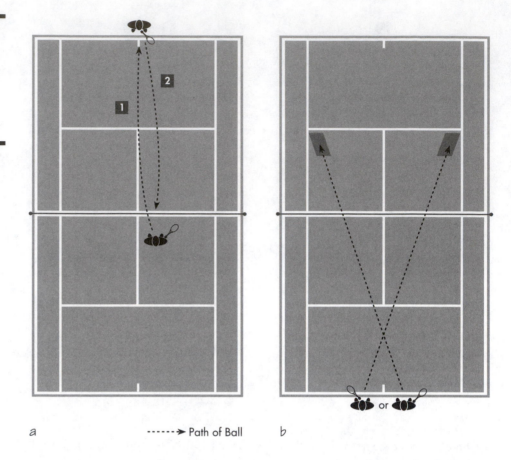

a   ------→ Path of Ball   b

EQUIPMENT

The axiom "you get what you pay for" is a useful phrase to remember when shopping for tennis equipment. Using the right equipment will help you improve your game and reduce the risk of injury. Shoes, socks, and rackets in particular should be selected with special care.

Footwear

Aside from cost and appearance, weight, comfort, and durability should be considered when purchasing tennis shoes. In most cases, the buyer should balance these three factors to get the best shoe. Heavier shoes are often the most durable but may not be comfortable due to the extra weight. The rule of thumb is to buy the lightest shoe possible once you are satisfied with the comfort, durability, cost, and appearance. Remember, tennis involves forward, backward, and sideward movements as well as sudden stops and starts. Check to see whether the shoe is likely to stand up well to these conditions.

The court surface played on and your style of play also help to determine the type of shoe to be purchased. People who play often on hard court surfaces may wear out shoes in several weeks. Others who play on softer surfaces may get months out of their shoes. Anticipate how much abuse the toe of the shoe will take. Some players, because of the tendency to drag the toe during groundstrokes, wear out one toe of the shoe completely while the rest of the shoe remains in good condition.

Avoid the urge to buy "imitation brand" tennis shoes from discount stores. These shoes are typically less durable and often promote blisters on the feet and ankles due to improper fit and wear. They also lack sufficient arch support, insole firmness, and support to the heel, which may lead to added stress to feet, ankles, and knees. Similarly, "jogging" or "cross-training" shoes should never be used on a tennis court. These shoes, because of their flared heels, tend to mark the court surface and are not constructed for lateral movement, therefore increasing the possibility of injury.

Socks

The abuse taken by the feet during a tennis match means that any pair of white gym socks may not be adequate. The key is to balance two important factors, absorbency and durability. Cotton or wool socks absorb more moisture from perspiration but acrylic/nylon blends wear longer. However, the acrylic/nylon blends tend to promote blisters faster because foot perspiration next to the skin is not absorbed, resulting in more foot movement within the sock. Some tennis equipment manufacturers market a tennis sock with acrylic on the inside and cotton out. The acrylic layer next to the foot draws the moisture away and into the cotton layer, where it is absorbed. The tennis socks also feature extra layers of fabric to cushion the foot. Many tennis players wear two pairs of socks to reduce blisters.

Clothing

Relaxation of the all-white tennis wear custom has meant an explosion in the tennis apparel industry in the last three decades. The benefit to the consumer, aside from appearance, has been a wide variety of shirts, shorts, skirts, and warm-ups. White is still popular today as the base color because of its ability to reflect, and not absorb, the sun's rays. Although styles will continue to change, most players dress for comfort first and fashion second. For example, larger-fitting shirts allow flexibility when serving without restriction from the clothing.

Rackets

Evidence of the change in the tennis racket industry may be found by examining the differences in size and composition of rackets over the years. Wood rackets, the standard for several decades, were replaced almost overnight by metal, which, in turn, were supplanted by composite brands. Racket head sizes have increased so that now the consumer may choose from standard, midsize, and oversize heads. The midsized tennis racket is 20 percent larger than the regular. The oversized racket is 30 percent larger than the original. The number and variety of brands available to the consumer have made the selection of a racket a most daunting task. However, a few basic principles can make the task relatively easy.

1. Quality costs money. Even though starter rackets can cost between $25 and $50, serious players often spend between $100 and $500 for their rackets. The difference in racket design, feel, and quality is not easily apparent to the beginner because of slick packaging by manufacturers. It may be wise to get a few recommendations from the tennis instructor before spending a large sum of money on a racket.

2. The larger the hitting surface, the larger the **sweet spot**—the area on the strings that provides the most powerful and accurate shot. Since a larger sweet spot also gives you the greatest chance to make solid contact, the midsize or oversize rackets are preferred, especially by beginners.

3. Composite rackets reduce the vibration—the rapid aftershock of the frame and strings—that is felt on contact with the ball. Composite rackets produce more powerful shots with less stress transferred to the elbow. Most composite rackets are a combination of graphite and fiberglass. The greater the percentage of graphite, the stiffer the racket.

sweet spot

4. Rackets are also classified according to weight, balance, flexibility, and grip size. All should be considered before selecting a racket.

Weight: Selection of the right "weight" racket is usually a matter of personal preference, although recent trends have been toward lighter rackets. A heavier racket generally means more power.

Balance: This can be checked by supporting the racket at its midpoint. An evenly balanced racket will rest horizontally; the head will rise on a head-light racket. Head-light rackets offer faster head speed for volleys and emergency situations and are preferred by most beginners. Head-heavy rackets may offer more power for some players.

Flexibility: This refers to how much "playability," or bend, the racket exhibits when the ball is hit. Stiff frames provide more power but transfer more of the force to the elbow joint area. Improper stroke mechanics combined with a stiff racket may be a cause of **tennis elbow.** Flexible rackets give players more control. Beginners should select a flexible racket first and possibly move to a stiffer racket once they have gained proficiency in shot making.

Grip Size: Perhaps the most important factor in racket selection is the grip or handle size. Handle grip circumferences vary by ⅛-inch increments. A 4¼ grip would likely be used by a small youth, a 4⅜ grip by an average size woman, and a 4¾ grip by a large man. Players may need to test several grip sizes before the correct one is found. A good tennis store will have "loaners" for trial use.

Another method for measuring grip size is to measure in inches the distance from the crease in your long palm (the second line below your fingers) to the tip of your ring finger (see figure 1.5). This distance corresponds to your grip size. To check for the correct grip size, hold the racket as you would hit the ball and have a partner twist the racket quickly forward and backward to simulate an off-center hit. If you can hold the handle firmly without it slipping in your hand, the grip is probably correct.

Although prestrung rackets are available at most tennis stores, many players buy unstrung racket frames and select the type of string and tension to suit their style of play. Beginners should select a nylon or other synthetic string with high durability. Top players may use animal **gut** strings, which have superior playing characteristics but shorter life. Recent distribution of synthetic gut string has been an attempt to combine the strength of gut with the durability of nylon. A string job typically costs between $10 and $40, depending on the string selected.

String tension recommendations are usually made by the manufacturer and are often printed on the shaft of the racket. Larger racket heads should be strung at between 72 and 80 pounds, midsize rackets between 55 and 65 pounds, and standard-size frames between 50 and 60 pounds. If one string breaks, all strings should be replaced.

Tennis Balls

Tennis balls, like rackets, vary considerably in quality. Good tennis balls will improve play and reduce the frustration of dealing with inconsistent bounces or uneven wear. Your tennis teacher can suggest several brands of high-quality tennis balls. Whatever the brand, look for the United States Tennis Association or International

tennis elbow

gut

Figure 1.5

Tennnis grip measurement from second line in palm to ring finger tip.

Tennis Federation seal of approval. When opening a can of tennis balls, the depressurization sound ("hiss") should be readily heard. Balls without adequate pressure upon opening are defective and should not be used. Balls with adequate pressure should rebound to waist level when dropped from eye level. Ball colors include white, yellow, orange, and fuchsia, with yellow being the color most easily seen and most often used.

Tennis balls last usually two to three matches or practice sessions. Balls unsuitable for play have lost their nap or felt and/or their bounce. Since tennis balls are usually purchased in cans of three balls, one of the more frustrating experiences for players is to play with one or more balls that "play" differently than the others. When this happens, break out a new can. The extra cost will be well worth the increased satisfaction experienced by both players. Worn-out tennis balls can still be used in "solo" practice sessions.

Heavy-duty permacore pressureless tennis balls are also available. These balls do not bounce as high, but they last longer than the pressurized type. Their durability make them an excellent choice for school classes or practice sessions. You can also buy special tennis balls to use at high altitudes.

The Game

A tennis **match** between two players is known as **singles. Doubles** is a match between four players—two on each team. **Mixed doubles** is match pairing a man and woman on one team against a similar combination on the other team.

A tennis match begins with a coin toss or spin of the racket to decide who serves first and on which ends of the court they will begin. One player serves and the point is played to its conclusion. Points are scored on every play and may be won by hitting a winner or by forcing the opponent to hit an error. Frequent errors include hitting out of bounds, into the net, or after the second bounce of the ball. After the serve, the ball may be hit out of the air or after one bounce on the court.

A server serves an entire **game,** alternating serves from the right and left sides of the **center mark** to the receiver. In singles, the **receiver** also moves from right to left to receive the serve. In doubles, the partners alternate turns as the receiver. This pattern continues until the game is won by one player or the other.

In singles, a server may serve and elect to play offensively, rushing to the net and trying to end the point quickly with a volley or overhead. This is known as serve and volley tennis. Players such as Pete Sampras and Jana Novotna typify the serve and volley style of tennis. On the other hand, a server may wish to remain near the **baseline** and hit groundstrokes hoping to force an error or simply outlast the opponent. This is called the **baseline game.** Steffi Graff and Michael Chang are excellent baseline players.

Once a server wins or loses a game, the opponent serves the next game. Thereafter, in singles, the players simply alternate games as the server. In doubles, a serving order is established whereby teams alternate servers. The serving order must be maintained throughout the entire set. An easy method of remembering the serving order is to recognize that a player will always serve from the same end of the court each time he or she serves. A **set** is won when one player or team has won at least six games and is ahead by at least two games. A set score might be 6-0, 6-2, 7-5, 8-6, or so on.

A match is won by the player or team who wins two out of three, or three out of five sets. There are also shorter variations of matches such as eight-game **pro sets,** which are used in tournaments when time is limited. In all matches, players

**match
singles
doubles
mixed doubles**

**game
center mark
receiver**

**baseline
baseline game**

set

pro sets

switch ends of the court when the total number of games played in a set is an odd number. This equalizes any court or weather differences for both players or teams.

In most matches, even in club tournament play, players keep their own scores and call their own lines. When a ball lands out of bounds, the player should call "out" and/or gesture with a hand signal. No sound from a player means the ball is inbounds and play should continue. Shots landing on the line are considered in. Tennis is a game that demands good sportsmanship. Proper etiquette for players calling lines suggests that unless the ball is clearly out, the ball should be considered in and play should continue. As tournament play becomes better and more formalized, umpires are often used to call the score and settle disputes. At the higher levels of play, linespersons are positioned around the court to call the lines.

RULES AND VIOLATIONS

Singles

The player who wins the toss may choose to serve or receive, or to play the first game on one end of the court or the other. If the player chooses to serve, the other player must receive serve in the first game and may choose either end of the court. Before beginning a match, all practice shots, including serves, should be completed.

The server stands behind the baseline and to the right of the center mark. In singles, only the singles sideline is used. The serve is directed across the net into the service court diagonally opposite the server. The server must not step on or inside the court boundary until after the ball is contacted. Doing so would result in a **foot fault.** The receiver should assume a position close to or on the baseline directly behind the appropriate service court. If the receiver makes an attempt at returning the ball, he or she is considered ready. The receiver must allow the ball to bounce once before returning it. If the ball lands on or inside the service court, the ball is returned and the play continues until the point is determined. If the ball is not good, the server gets a **second serve,** or chance, to get the ball into the service court. If both serves result in errors, a **double fault** results in the point being awarded to the receiver.

After each point is played, the server and the receiver line up on the other sides of the center mark to begin the next point. A **let serve** occurs when the ball hits the top of the net and lands legally on or within the proper service court. A let serve entitles the server to repeat the serve without penalty.

foot fault

second serve
double fault

let serve

Doubles

The doubles server normally stands further from the center mark than in singles because the server's partner is able to intercept a **down-the-line shot** that may otherwise result in a winner. The doubles sideline is now in play, meaning teams must now cover the **alley.** Players on the serving team decide who will serve first. Generally, the stronger server serves first, although weather conditions such as sun and wind may be factors, especially if one player is left-handed. The receivers should also decide who will return on the right and left sides, respectively. Like the serving order, receivers must also receive from the same sides throughout the set. The scoring system applies equally to singles and doubles play.

down-the-line shot

alley

COURT DIMENSIONS AND MARKINGS

Figure 2.1 illustrates the lines, areas, dimensions, and markings of a tennis court.

Figure 2.1

Court lines, markings, and areas.

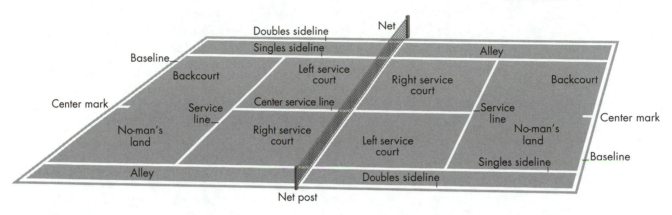

SCORING

A game in tennis requires at least four points to win. The game score is called in large numbers (15, 30, 40, etc.) because of the game's history and because of the need to differentiate it from the set score, which is scored in small numbers (1, 2, 3, etc.). A zero score is called **love**. The server's score is always announced first. The first point is 15, the second, 30, and the third, 40. A player may win the game on the next point after 40 if he or she has a two-point advantage over the opponent.

love

A score of 30–15 would indicate that the server had won two points and the receiver one point. Two points each would be called 30 all. At 40–40, the term **deuce** (tie) is used. Thereafter, one player gains the advantage by scoring a point. If the server gains the **advantage** the score is called **ad in.** Should the receiver gain the advantage, the score is **ad out.** The game can return to deuce if the player who is behind gains the next point, or be won by the player who is ahead if he or she scores the next point. Consequently, each game must be won by a margin of at least two points. For this reason, games matching equal opponents may last for some time. Use table 2.1 as a handy reference guide for learning the scoring system.

deuce

advantage
ad in
ad out

Some tournaments use **no ad** scoring to speed up the game. In this type of scoring, the winner must win only four points. The points are called 1, 2, 3, and 4 rather than the traditional scoring, and there are no ads. If the score reaches 3 all, the receiver has the choice of service courts in which to receive the serve.

no ad

The set score refers to the number of games each player or team has won. Once again, the server's score is always announced first. A set score of 1–5 would indicate that the server has won only one game to the receiver's five. A set is won by the player who wins six games and has at least a two-game margin over the opponent. Possible set scores might be 6–0 to 6–4, 7–5, 8–6, and so on. During the Wimbledon Championships in England, two players once recorded a set score of 30–28. So that tournament matches might better fit within television time periods, a twelve-point **tiebreaker** system was adopted by the USTA. Tiebreakers have added much drama to championship matches. The first server in the tiebreaker is the player who would have served in the next game. The server delivers the first serve of the tiebreaker from the right of the center mark. The second player then serves points 2 and 3 from the left, then right sides, respectively. The first player serves points 4 and 5 from the left and right sides, and so on until the sixth point is played, at which time the players change sides of the net and resume play. The tiebreaker is continued in this manner until one player gets seven points and is

tiebreaker

TABLE 2.1	Guide to tennis scoring system		
SERVER	**RECEIVER**	**SCORE**	**SERVE FROM**
0 points	0 points	love–all	right
1 point	0 points	15–love*	left
0 points	1 point	love–15*	left
1 point	1 point	15–all*	right
2 points	0 points	30–love	right
0 points	2 points	love–30	right
2 points	1 point	30–15	left
1 point	2 points	15–30	left
2 points	2 points	30–all	right
3 points	0 points	40–love	left
0 points	3 points	love–40	left
3 points	1 point	40–15	right
1 point	3 points	15–40	right
3 points	2 points	40–30	left
2 points	3 points	30–40	left
3 points	3 points	deuce	right
4 points	0, 1, or 2	game to server	
0, 1, 2	4 points	game to receiver	

*The first point, 15, is sometimes informally called 5 for brevity.

ahead by at least two points. A set decided by a tiebreaker is recorded as 7-6. The player or team that served first in the tiebreaker receives the serve in the first game of the next set. Use table 2.2 as a reference guide for learning the tiebreaker serving system.

ETIQUETTE

Tennis was traditionally a gentlemen's game. Even today, you won't find chanting crowds, acrobatic cheerleaders, or marching bands at most tennis matches. Regardless of whether you are a player, coach, or spectator, you will be held to a higher standard of conduct. Tennis spectators are typically more reserved and polite. They frequently applaud good play but rarely make derisive comments. Tennis players are expected to treat their opponents fairly and to show good sportsmanship and proper etiquette at all times.

Spectator Etiquette

The key to being a good spectator is to not interrupt the concentration of the players on the court. Loud noises or unnecessary conversation should be avoided. Extraneous movements should be made between, not during, points. Likewise, applause is welcomed after, not during, play. Spectators should not converse with the players during a match. Trying to find out the score of the match by asking a player is not good etiquette. Spectators should get up to move to other courts only when players change sides of the court, never during play or between points. If you are walking to another court and must pass a court where a match is in progress,

TABLE 2.2	Guide to twelve-point tiebreaker system	
POINT	**PLAYER A**	**PLAYER B**
1	serve from right	receive
2	receive	serve from left
3	receive	serve from right
4	serve from left	receive
5	serve from right	receive
6	receive	serve from left
After the 6th point players		switch sides of net
7	receive	serve from right
8	serve from left	receive
9	serve from right	receive
10	receive	serve from left
11	receive	serve from right
12	serve from left	receive

If necessary, this pattern continues until the tiebreaker is decided by a two-point margin.

walk inconspicuously behind the fence of the court after the conclusion of the point in progress.

Player Etiquette

Players should be courteous to opponents at all times. When you meet a player for the first time, it is customary to introduce yourself and shake hands. Offer to spin the racket or toss a coin to determine the serving order and the sides of the court to be defended by each. Before starting warm-up, make sure you have all necessary equipment, including a backup racket in case a string breaks. Bring a water container to stay hydrated during the match.

Once the warm-up begins, allow the opponent to practice all shots desired. Complete the warm-up within the prescribed time allotted by the tournament committee or within about 10 minutes if an informal match. Practice serves should be taken before the match begins. Playing the "first one in" is not appropriate.

Once the match begins, allow your opponent time to get ready before serving. Hurrying your opponent is not good sportsmanship and experienced players will recognize and avoid falling prey to this tactic. Servers should have two balls ready for play. Leaving one ball at the back of the court for the second serve is not acceptable. Should the server be holding two balls, and the first serve is good, the second ball must not be thrown away onto the court surface. A second ball on the court constitutes a **let** and the point is replayed. The best practice is to wear shorts with pockets for the extra ball so that it does not interfere with play.

let

Players should avoid the foot-fault rule even when playing without an umpire. Although it is not good etiquette to call a player on a foot fault, it is also unacceptable for the server to take unfair advantage by consistently violating the rule. Servers should announce the score just prior to serving so that both players keep up to date on the progress of the game. This helps to avoid later disputes about the score. If a serve is an obvious **fault,** it is not good etiquette to hit the ball back over the net to the opponent or to practice a return. The ball should be hit under control

fault

into the net, let go past the baseline, or caught and pocketed. If the receiver returns a ball you thought was out, play should continue as if the ball were in.

After every point, receivers have an obligation to return balls on their side of the court to the server promptly and accurately. If a ball has gone onto another court, wait until play on that court stops, and then ask to have the ball returned. Players should never run onto another court to retrieve a ball while play is in progress. Thanking players on neighboring courts for returning balls is always appreciated.

During play, give your opponent the benefit of the doubt on all line calls. You are responsible for calling the lines on your side of the court, but not your opponent's. If you are not sure about a call, consider the ball in and award the opponent the point. In informal play, it is acceptable to ask the opponent to make the call if you were obstructed or did not see the ball land. Call balls out loud and clear but do not call balls that are in. Out calls should be made immediately or the ball is presumed in.

Touching the net, double hitting, or carrying the ball should be called by the player who makes the infraction. If a ball rolls onto your court, call a let, and re-play the point. Balls left on the court are considered part of the court surface. Not only are they a safety hazard, they may cause you to lose a point if inadvertently hit by an opponent.

Controlling one's temper in tennis is often difficult in competitive situations, yet should be done as much as possible. As well, criticizing doubles partners is not acceptable behavior. Opponents and partners alike should be complimented for well-played shots. When a match has ended, players should congratulate each other by shaking hands. Excuses offered for poor play are not generally welcomed.

When leaving the court, take all balls and other debris with you. A good rule of thumb is to leave the court in better condition than you found it. If others are waiting for a court, show courtesy by offering to play doubles or by limiting your play to one set or 30 minutes.

Some tennis clubs maintain dress and/or behavior codes. Be sure to observe these requirements. Good sportsmanship and etiquette on the part of players and spectators alike can make a tennis match an enjoyable experience for all.

Skills and Drills

INTRODUCTION

skills
elements

Tennis is a game of many **skills.** Serves, groundstrokes, and volleys are just a few examples. Each skill is composed of various parts or **elements** that, if executed correctly, contribute to successful performance of the skill. For example, when hitting a groundstroke, bringing the racket back early in preparation for the shot and following through after contact with the ball are two elements of the skill that make for a good groundstroke. Elements, then, are the foundation of your game. Without them, the foundation cannot stand. By learning and practicing the elements that make up the skills of tennis, a player can build a solid foundation that contributes to effective performance on the court.

This section presents the skills of tennis. Each skill is broken down into its different elements. Each element is described in detail with key phrases serving as cues to facilitate learning. How the element fits into the skill as well as its overall importance to the game are discussed. Finally, several drills that will help to incorporate the elements into your repertoire are provided.

SKILL 1   Getting Ready to Hit

Tennis players do not just swing at the ball as it comes by; they must perform several elements to get ready to execute the stroke. They must hold the racket properly. They must put the body in a position that allows them quick and efficient movement. They must efficiently move to where the ball will be stroked. They must move the body and the racket into the correct position to execute the stroke. When all of these elements have been mastered, a successful stroke can occur. If even one of these elements is performed incorrectly, however, an error often results. The majority of errors in tennis are related not to the stroke itself but to one or more of the elements involved. For example, a beginning player may not get the racket back soon enough to play the ball. This is one of many such important elements that need to be learned.

The Grip

The beginning tennis player will not be accustomed to hitting a ball with an extra 27 inches of length in the hand. The hand-eye coordination developed in performing skills such as catching a ball will need to be modified somewhat because of this extra length. Fortunately, this adjustment is not that difficult. The sooner the racket feels like an extension of the hand, the sooner the player will develop control.

Developing control starts with the hands. More specifically, the fingers hold the racket and are what ultimately develop control. Much like a carpenter develops the feel of the hammer when skillfully driving nails into wood, the beginning tennis player should practice feeling the ball on the strings when learning the grip. Practice holding the racket firmly and then tightening the grip just before contact is made with the ball. If the racket is not held firmly, the force of the ball hitting the strings will cause the racket to turn in the hand. Learn to apply pressure to the handle primarily with the index and middle fingers. For more control, there should be a gap between these two fingers. Relaxing the fingers between shots will allow you to change grips easier.

A tennis racket is held with a grip that allows the racket face to contact the ball basically in a perpendicular position to the direction of its flight. Because strokes are made on both forehand and backhand sides in tennis, and the technique for hitting each stroke is different, the forehand and backhand grips need to be different also.

Forehand Grip

eastern forehand

There are three forehand grips used by tennis players. The **eastern forehand,** or "shake-hands" grip, is the most common and is achieved by shaking hands with the handle while the racket head is perpendicular to the ground or standing on edge (see figure 3.1a). The "V" formed by the thumb and index finger is squarely on the top of the racket handle. Technically, the eastern forehand is easier to master for beginning and intermediate players because of its ability to place the racket head at a direct right angle to the flight of the ball.

continental grip

The **continental grip** is a more-advanced grip used by some top players. In this grip, the palm of the hand shifts more toward the top of the racket (see figure 3.1b). This permits the player to use the continental grip for both forehand and backhand strokes. Players who prefer not to change grips, and who slice their backhands, may find this grip to their liking. The main disadvantage of the continental grip is having to move the wrist backward slightly to play the ball in front of the forward foot.

topspin
western forehand

Players who play primarily from the baseline and who want to impart more **topspin** on the ball may use the **western forehand** grip to advantage. In this grip,

Figure 3.1

Tennis grips.

a

b

Left-hand
eastern
forehand grip

Right-hand
eastern
forehand grip

Right-hand
continental
grip

Left-hand
continental
grip

Figure 3.1
Continued.

c

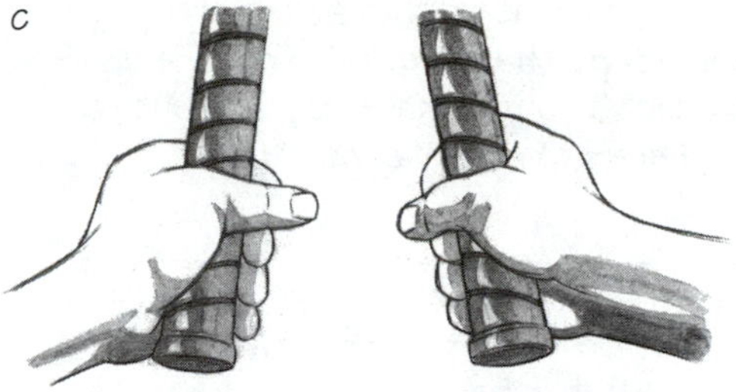

Left-hand western forehand grip

Right-hand western forehand grip

d

Right-hand eastern backhand grip

Left-hand eastern backhand grip

e

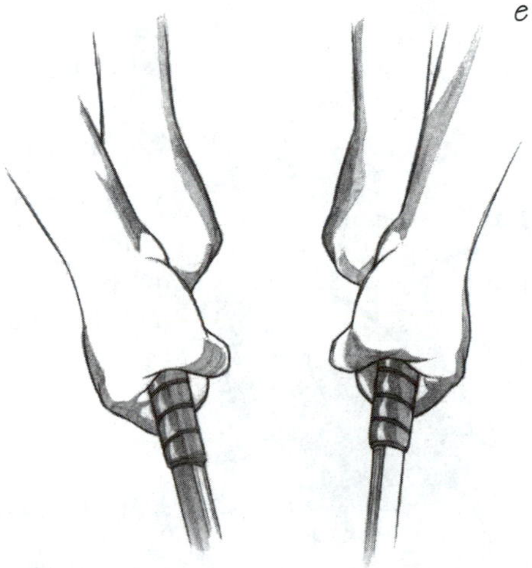

Right-hand two-handed backhand grip

Left-hand two-handed backhand grip

the palm moves more underneath the racket handle (see figure 3.1c). Many clay court specialists use the western forehand grip.

Backhand Grip

Traditionally, the **eastern backhand** has been the most common backhand grip (see figure 3.1d), although the two-handed backhand grip has gained worldwide prominence in the last twenty-five years. The eastern backhand, like its forehand counterpart, allows the player to hit the ball well ahead of the front foot while keeping the correct angle of the racket head to the ball. The palm of the hand rests on top of the handle in this grip. The thumb braces the side of the handle.

The success of **two-handed backhand** players such as Chris Evert and Bjorn Borg changed the perception of the backhand as primarily a defensive stroke to that of a powerful weapon. In terms of the grip, the two-handed backhand offers an obvious increase in support because of the extra hand on the handle. The palm of the lower hand on the two-handed backhand grip rests on top of the handle while the palm of the upper hand rests on the side of the handle (see figure 3.1e). This arrangement maximizes stability although there is a reduced range of motion.

Changing grips involves using the nonracket hand (held at the throat of the racket) to turn the racket. The grip is loosened during this process, then quickly tightened with the new grip in place immediately before the forward swing is made. Players should spend time practicing grip changes until they become routine (see figure 3.2).

eastern backhand

two-handed backhand

Figure 3.2
Changing your grip.

CUE: Develop the habit of bringing the free hand up to cradle the throat of the racket after each shot. This keeps the racket in a neutral position and allows you to make adjustments to your grip before the next shot.

Drills for Practicing the Grip

#1: Hammer Drill

Assume the eastern forehand grip on the racket handle. With the edge of the racket closest to the court surface, pretend you are hammering a nail into the court with the racket. Hammer for 30 seconds and then change to the backhand grip and repeat.

CUE: Hammer it in.

#2: Ball Dribble Drill

Use an eastern forehand grip and bounce the ball on the court as many times as possible without changing the grip (see figure 3.3). Practice absorbing the ball by lifting the racket slightly after each contact. Perform 30 consecutive bounces. For added difficulty, alternate sides of the racket on each bounce.

CUE: Absorb the ball.

#3: Air Ball Dribble Drill

Use an eastern forehand grip and turn the palm up. Bounce the ball a few inches into the air with the strings (see figure 3.4). Try to land the ball on the center of the strings each time. Perform 30 consecutive bounces. For added difficulty, try alternating sides of the racket for each bounce.

Figure 3.3
Ball dribble drill (a).

Figure 3.4
Air ball dribble drill (b).

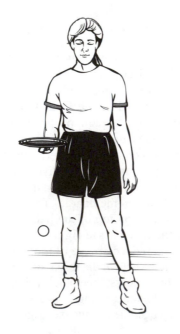

a

b

CUE: *"Aim for the center of the strings."*

#4: Grip Check Drill

Stand about 3 feet behind the baseline. Use an eastern forehand grip, step forward to swing at an imaginary ball coming from across the net. Stop at the hypothetical contact point with the ball and check to see that the racket head is directly above and parallel to the baseline. Perform 10 correct grip placements, then change to backhand grip.

#5: Tennis Ball Pickup Drill

Try these methods of picking the ball up without using the free hand:

a. Move the ball with the racket next to the inside of the foot. Press the ball against the foot with the racket and lift up quickly. Bounce the ball once with the strings into your free hand.

b. Same as a., except use the outside of your foot.

c. Place the racket head on top of the ball and slide it quickly toward you. As the ball begins moving toward you, quickly slide the racket head underneath the ball and scoop it up and into your free hand.

d. Start dribbling a ball on the court by slapping it with the racket once, then lifting the racket up quickly. As the ball rises from the ground, bounce it once or twice until the ball is high enough to gather it in with the free hand.

Perform each method 3 times while using the eastern forehand grip.

#6: Bounce with Racket Edge Drill

Bounce the ball repeatedly onto the court using only the racket edge. A variation is to bounce the ball into the air using only the racket edge. For added difficulty, alternate air and court bounces. Perform 5 consecutive bounces using the eastern forehand grip.

#7: Becker Bounce Drill (BBD)

This drill was made famous by Boris Becker. Choke up so that the hand loosely cradles the throat of the racket. Using low bounces, angle the bounce of the ball forward and back while walking to the net. Bounce the ball to the net without losing control. This drill is for learning to control the ball with the racket, not for practice of the grip.

The Ready Position

Being in a good ready position is an important element of hitting a groundstroke because in most cases the player must move to where the ball must be stroked. Often the player does not know whether the ball will come to the forehand or backhand side until the moment the shot is played by the opponent. The player must therefore be in a balanced position that allows quick movement in any direction. A good **ready position** is performed by keeping the knees slightly bent with the weight forward on the balls of the feet, a slight forward bend at the waist with the racket held in front of the body (see figure 3.5). The player should be watching the opponent carefully, trying to pick up any information that might indicate where the ball will be hit before it is actually contacted.

ready position

Figure 3.5
Ready position.

Moving to Hit the Ball

Since most shots are hit either on the run or, preferably, after running to the ball and setting up, being able to move effectively is a requisite element for successful tennis. Movement to the ball begins with the player unweighting, like a skier who shifts his or her weight to turn on skis, then running toward the ball.

After unweighting, movement to the ball is either a shuffle step for close shots or a cross-step and run for farther shots (see figure 3.6). Setting up for the shot involves planting the back foot as a brake, then pivoting and stepping toward the net. Practicing this movement sequence is a key to good footwork.

CUE: Teachers often use the phrase "hurry and wait" as a reminder to quickly move to the correct position to hit the ball rather than attempting to time arrival with that of the ball.

Drills for Practicing Movement to the Ball

#8: Unweight and Shuffle Drill

Start in the ready position about 8 to 10 feet from a line. Unweight by bending then straightening the knees, then shuffle sideways and touch the line with the foot. Do not cross the feet during the shuffle step.

#9: Unweight, Turn, and Run Drill

From the ready position, unweight, then pivot, turn, and run to a line about 12 to 15 feet away.

#10: Ball Pickup Shuffle Drill

Place tennis balls 10 feet apart across the court. Start in the ready position on the doubles sideline. Using the shuffle step, move to the first ball, pick it up and return

Figure 3.6
Court movement.

a   Shuffle

b   Cross-step and run

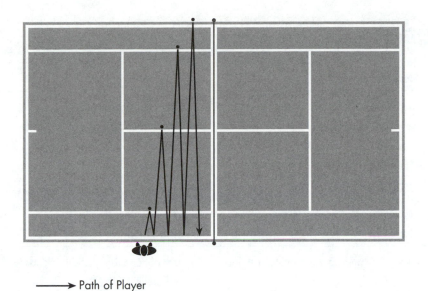

Figure 3.7
Ball pickup shuffle drill.

———▶ Path of Player

it to the doubles sideline (see figure 3.7). Shuffle to the second ball and return it to the spot where the first ball was placed. Continue this pattern until all balls have been picked up and moved.

#11: Ball Pickup Turn and Run Drill

Place the balls 15 to 20 feet apart. The actions are the same as in the ball pickup shuffle drill, except the player should turn and run to the ball.

#12: Roll the Ball Drill

Have a partner roll balls continuously to each corner of the service court (see figure 3.8). Roll each ball back and shuffle across the **service line** to retrieve the next one. The partner should roll the next ball just as the first ball is released by the player. Keep the pattern going as long as possible.

Table 3.1 summarizes the key elements and common errors in getting ready to hit.

service line

Figure 3.8
Roll the ball drill.

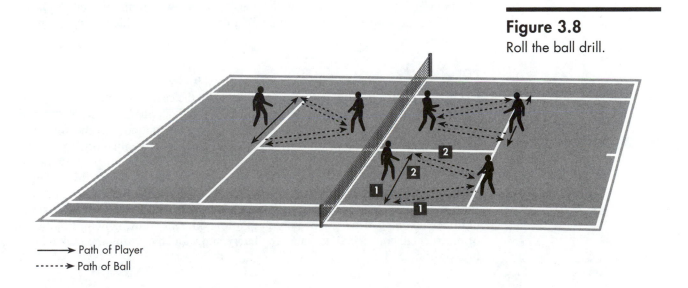

———▶ Path of Player
------▶ Path of Ball

TABLE 3.1	Key elements and common errors: Getting ready to hit

READY POSITION	
Key Elements	**Common Errors**
1. Weight evenly balanced	1. Not in ready position
2. Forehand or backhand grip	2. Guide hand not on throat of racket
3. Knees bent	3. Incorrect or inconsistent grip selection
4. Guide hand on throat of racket	

MOVING TO HIT THE BALL	
Key Elements	**Common Errors**
1. Unweight by pushing down on court surface, then move	1. Lack of good ready position leads to slow unweighting/first step
2. Shuffle-step for close shots	2. Times arrival with that of the ball
3. Turn and run for far shots	3. Moves and hits at same time
4. Hurry and wait for ball	4. Watches ball instead of opponent after shot
5. Focus on opponent's return after ball is played	
6. Return to central court position after shot	

SKILL 2 | Groundstrokes

groundstroke
forehand groundstroke

backhand groundstroke

A **groundstroke** is a shot hit after the ball bounces on the court. A **forehand groundstroke** is hit on the right side of the body for a right-handed player. It is used more than any other stroke in tennis and thus is an important skill. Because it is hit on the same side of the body as the dominant hand, the forehand groundstroke is generally easier to learn than the backhand. The **backhand groundstroke** is played on the left side of the body for a right-handed player and may involve a one- or two-handed grip of the racket. The backhand is generally considered a more difficult stroke to learn, although some players actually find it a more natural motion. A common strategy for players is to exploit an opponent's backhand by playing to it because it is generally the weaker of the two groundstrokes. A player with a well-developed backhand has a valuable weapon with which to win points.

Forehand

Using one of the forehand grips (most players use the eastern forehand), the player assumes the ready position while waiting for the opponent to return the ball (see figure 3.9). As soon as the player knows the ball is going to the forehand side, the player begins the preparation phase. The backswing initiates the preparation phase and begins with the player moving the racket back either in a straight line parallel to the court or in a looping motion to a position where the racket is about waist height and pointing to the fence behind the court. A frequent problem for beginning players is that they wait until after the ball has bounced before starting the backswing. This practice does not allow time for adjustments for ball spin or unexpected bounces. Remember to "hurry and wait" by getting the racket back into position early.

Figure 3.9
Forehand groundstroke.

a Eastern forehand grip

b Early backswing and pivot

c Step toward target

d Contact even with front foot

e Follow through

The ball should ideally be played at about waist level, thus it is important for the player to make small adjustments with the feet to get the body into the correct position as much as possible. As the ball approaches, pointing the opposite shoulder toward the ball helps to turn the body sideways to the net. This puts the body into a position where the use of **angular momentum** can add power to the shot. Angular momentum is created by turning the upper torso to face the net as the ball is stroked. The weight is moved forward by stepping forward toward the oncoming ball. The step forward adds **linear momentum** to the shot. Without the body turn and weight transfer, the only source of power will be from the arm, which is inefficient and causes the arm to tire quickly.

During the forward swing, the racket should be parallel to the court through the hitting zone where the ball is contacted. The swing should occur after the step forward. The swing motion is performed with a firm wrist. In other words, the wrist should be tensed prior to contact with the ball so that it does not flex during the swing. To emphasize the firm arm and wrist position necessary during the forward swing, teachers often tell students to "sweep the table." Some beginning tennis players go too far, attempting to "choke" the racket by squeezing the grip too hard, thereby losing the feel of the ball on the strings.

CUE: To avoid holding the racket too loosely, squeeze the handle just as you begin the forward swing.

In the follow-through phase, the racket should follow the path of the ball created by the forward swing for as long as comfortably possible, then finish high to impart topspin on the ball. Topspin raises the trajectory of the ball over the net, keeps the ball in, and causes a high bounce for the opponent.

Refer to table 3.2 for a summary of the key elements and common errors for the forehand groundstroke.

Several different circumstances in tennis, such as unexpected bounces, wind, or ball spin, call for adjustments to be made when hitting groundstrokes. It is important to remember to try and keep the swinging motion as similar as possible and to make adjustments in other ways. For example, for a low bouncing ball, bend the knees so that the racket head doesn't have to be dropped down. For high bouncing balls, retreat quickly, brake with the back foot, then step forward and swing through. Here, too, the cue "hurry and wait" has particular relevance, because a player who has moved quickly into position has more time to react to unusual circumstances.

One-Handed Backhand

The eastern backhand is the most common grip used to play the one-handed backhand. With the eastern backhand grip, the V formed by the thumb and index finger should be slightly to the left of the top of the racket handle. Because players

TABLE 3.2   Key elements and common errors: Forehand groundstroke
BACKSWING PHASE

Key Elements	**Common Errors**
1. Eastern grip	1. Wrong grip, shots travel high over net and out
2. Racket back early	2. Waits until ball bounces to start backswing
3. Turn body sideways	3. No step forward
4. Step toward target	4. Backswing too long

FORWARD-SWING PHASE

Key Elements	**Common Errors**
1. Weight shift forward	1. Weight back on heels
2. Squeeze racket handle	2. Racket handle turns in hand on contact with ball
3. Hold wrist firm	3. Angle at elbow incorrect, arm too straight or bent
4. Contact ball opposite front foot	

FOLLOW-THROUGH PHASE

Key Elements	**Common Errors**
1. Swing through at target	1. Does not follow through at target, resulting in inaccurate shot
2. Swing out and finish high	
3. Return to ready position after shot	

normally have the forehand grip on the racket while waiting to play a ground-stroke, the grip must be changed to the backhand once it has been determined that a backhand groundstroke will be played. This is accomplished by having the left hand (for a right-handed player) lightly cradle the throat of the racket. The fore-hand grip is loosened, the racket turned slightly with the right hand, then the grip (now backhand) is tightened on the handle.

As in the forehand groundstroke, early preparation is an important prerequi-site to an effective backhand groundstroke. As the racket is brought back and the grip changed from forehand to backhand, the shoulder should turn toward the left sideline (see figure 3.10). This action places the back facing the net and al-

Figure 3.10
Backhand groundstroke.

a Turn shoulder

b Draw racket out
    of sheath

c Contact ahead
    of front foot

d Keep head down
    on contact

e

f

lows for angular momentum to add power to the shot. The step forward should be toward the net, again to add power via linear momentum. One of the most common mistakes that beginning players make is to open the stance too early by lifting the shoulder closest to the net. This action moves the body weight back onto the rear foot, usually resulting in control problems. Keeping the shoulder down allows the weight to be transferred forward and a controlled, powerful backhand executed.

The forward swing is generally made parallel to the court with the racket head higher than the wrist on all but the very low shots. The ball should be contacted just ahead of the front foot after the forward step toward the net has been made. You should be looking over the right shoulder as you begin the forward swing.

CUE: When performing the forward swing, think of drawing a sword out of a sheath.

Following through toward the target keeps the ball under control and adds power to the shot. Think of hitting not one but five or six balls all lined up in a row pointing at the target. This will keep you following through the ball longer.

CUE: To emphasize the follow-through, pretend to "pose for the camera" after a shot. This phrase helps you to think about following through after each shot.

Two-Handed Backhand

The two-handed backhand has become a very popular groundstroke in recent years and is an effective weapon for many players. Younger players may find that they lack the strength necessary to handle a one-handed backhand, yet they are able to readily adapt to the two-handed backhand. Some believe it is easier to learn than the one-handed backhand because of its similarity to the forehand. Most agree that the two-hander is a more powerful stroke because of the additional trunk rotation possible. Although some people have downplayed the two-handed backhand because of its lack of reach, players have compensated for this limitation by using one-handed shots for low-bouncing balls and other difficult-to-reach shots. Clearly, the two-handed backhand has many advantages. However, players need to experiment with both types to see which works best for them.

Holding the racket for the two-handed backhand is similar to holding a baseball bat. Using an eastern forehand grip with the dominant hand, bring the other hand up next to it, also with a forehand grip. Some players prefer to hold a regular backhand grip with the dominant hand and then use a forehand grip with the other. Either is acceptable; the key is comfort and getting the racket face in a square position to meet the oncoming ball.

Fundamentally, the two-handed and one-handed backhands are alike, except that the ball is played closer to the body with the two-handed backhand. Using the two-handed backhand to impart topspin can make a backhand groundstroke into a potent weapon. To add topspin, start the racket head from a lower position, somewhere between the hip and knee, then swing with an upward trajectory through the ball. To place backspin on a backhand groundstroke, start the racket head in a higher-than-waist position and swing through the ball with a downward trajectory (see figure 3.11).

Table 3.3 summarizes the key elements and common errors in the backhand groundstroke.

TABLE 3.3	Key elements and common errors: Backhand groundstroke

BACKSWING PHASE

Key Elements	Common Errors
1. Eastern or two-handed grip	1. Wrong grip, shots travel high over net and out
2. Point racket at back fence	2. Waits until ball bounces to start backswing
3. Turn sideways, look over shoulder	
4. Step toward target	

FORWARD-SWING PHASE

Key Elements	Common Errors
1. Weight shift forward	1. Leads with elbow
2. Squeeze racket handle	2. Weight back on heels
3. Hold wrist firm	3. Late in hitting ball, shots travel to the side
4. Contact ball just ahead of front foot	4. No power in shot because weight is not shifted forward

FOLLOW-THROUGH PHASE

Key Elements	Common Errors
1. Swing through at target	1. Does not follow through at target, resulting in lack of accuracy
2. Keep shoulders down while swinging out and finishing high	2. Lifts shoulders as contact is made; shots travel high and out
3. Return to ready position after shot	

Figure 3.11
Two-handed backhand.

Groundstroke Drills

#13: Groundstroke Mirror Drill

Players stand at the baseline facing the net. From the ready position, they execute the forehand and backhand groundstrokes without the ball, concentrating on each element of the stroke—grip, footwork, backswing, forward swing, and follow-through.

#14: Drop and Hit Drill

Players stand with their backs to the net and drop and hit to their partners at the baseline (see figure 3.12). Balls should be stroked easily with good form. Players should concentrate on dropping the ball out to the side and in front of the body to allow for the swing. Baseline players toss the ball back.

Figure 3.12
Drop and hit drill.

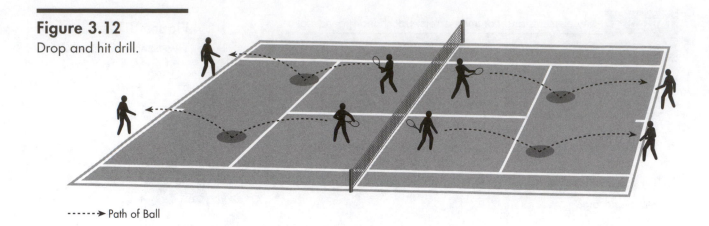

------▶ Path of Ball

#15: Toss and Hit Drill

Players at the baseline toss the ball underhand so that it bounces about halfway between partners (see figure 3.13). Partners start in the ready position with their backs facing the net. Hitters move quickly to the ball, stop, turn, step toward the ball, and swing, stroking the ball under control back to their partners. Partners catch the ball and repeat. They perform 5 to 10 forehand groundstrokes, then switch to backhands. Players then rotate.

#16: Railroad Tracks Drill

This drill is good for learning how far away you must be from the ball when stroking it. One player stands straddling the singles sideline with back to the net (see figure 3.14). A partner at the baseline tosses a ball down the doubles sideline so that it bounces roughly halfway between the players. The player at the net executes the four-step sequence and hits the ball back to the partner using the forehand groundstroke. The ball is hit above the doubles sideline while the feet are on the singles sideline.

#17: Run and Hit Drill

Hitters stand with their back to the net and face their partners who are at the baseline (see figure 3.15). The ball is tossed to the side of the hitters who must then run to the ball and hit it back to the partners. Players should practice hitting both forehands and backhands before rotating positions.

Figure 3.13
Toss and hit drill.

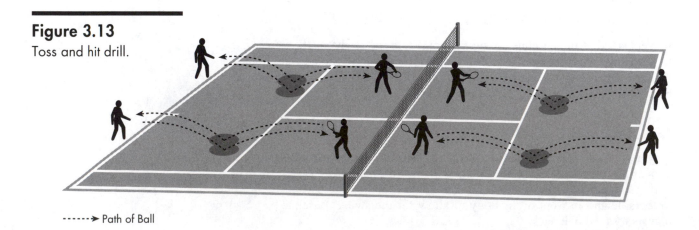

------▶ Path of Ball

Figure 3.14
Railroad tracks drill.

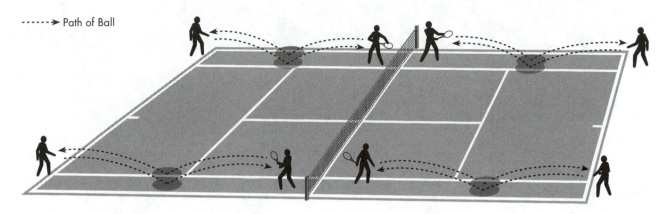

- - - - -▶ Path of Ball

#18: Groundstroke Rally Drill

With both players at their respective baselines, the ball is hit back and forth across the net continuously using forehand and backhand groundstrokes.

#19: Stay Deep Drill

Both players imagine the net is 6 feet high. Players **rally** back and forth by hitting the ball high over the net so that it lands between the service and baselines (see figure 3.16). Count one point for each ball that lands short of the service line.

rally

The Approach Shot

The **approach shot** is an offensive shot, played so that the player can move quickly to the net and gain the offensive position. A general rule of thumb is not to play an approach shot unless the ball has bounced short of the service line. When hitting the approach shot, move up to and beside the ball and prepare the racket early. As contact is made, follow through toward the target while holding the feet in position,

approach shot

Figure 3.15
Run and hit drill.

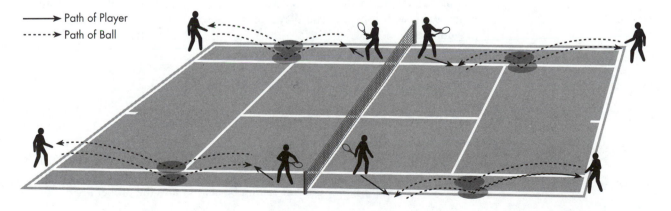

──────▶ Path of Player
- - - - -▶ Path of Ball

Figure 3.16
Stay deep drill.

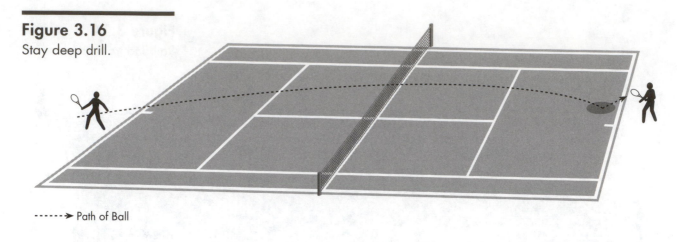

------→ Path of Ball

Figure 3.17
Approach shot drill.

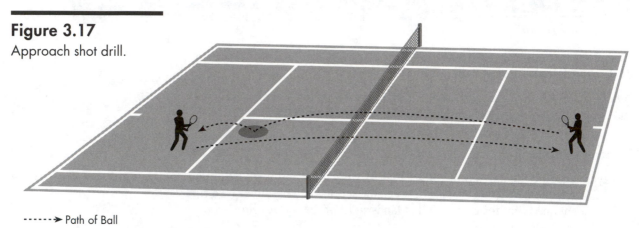

------→ Path of Ball

then start to move forward toward the net. A mistake many players make is to move the feet toward the net at the same time the ball is being played. This usually results in errors. On the forehand, an approach shot is usually played with topspin; on the backhand, backspin is usually used. Most approach shots are hit down the line, although this tactic should be balanced somewhat with hitting to the opponent's weaker side.

#20: Approach Shot Drill

Players rally back and forth across the net waiting for a short ball that bounces before the service line. When the opportunity arises, the player moves up on the ball and hits an approach shot either down-the-line (see figure 3.17) with underspin or **crosscourt** with topspin. The player then continues to the net and the point is played out.

crosscourt

SKILL 3 Serve and Serve Return

Beginner's (Punch) Serve

The serve is used to begin each point and can be a valuable weapon to possess at all levels of tennis. The beginning tennis player will find that the most critical element of the beginner's serve (also called a punch serve) is control. At this stage, velocity is not important if the ball cannot be served into the proper service court.

Once the player progresses to the point where the ball can be consistently served in, more attention may be given to developing the more powerful full serve. At all levels of tennis, however, accurate placement of the serve is the key to its use as an effective weapon.

The beginner's serve should be executed using the eastern forehand grip. Assume a 45-degree angle just behind the baseline and about a foot to the right or left of the center mark. Your feet should be about 6 to 12 inches apart. A method of consistently setting the position correctly is to point the front foot at the left net post (for a right-handed server). Let the back foot assume a comfortable position parallel with the baseline. Bend the knees slightly.

Hold one tennis ball (the second ball should be in your pocket) between the thumb and fingers, not in the palm of the hand. There is better control with the fingers. The toss should be made slightly higher than you can reach with your racket. Think of the toss as "placing the ball into position," instead of throwing the ball. This is most effectively done by drawing the letter "J" (or the letter "L" for a left-handed server) in the air with the toss arm. Keeping the toss arm basically straight, start the arm in front of and to the left of the body. Bring it down, across the body, and straight up as if drawing the J in the air. Release the ball carefully at the top of the J by simply opening up the fingers. The arm momentum generated is usually sufficient to achieve enough height in the toss, negating the need for additional force applied from the hand or fingers. Indeed, applying the force only with a straight arm is an important element in a consistent toss. Developing a consistent toss is really a simple matter of mathematics. If force is applied from the arm, wrist, and fingers (and, heaven forbid, the legs), there are three or four sources of potential error; with force applied from the arm only, there is just one. Learning to toss consistently is therefore much easier.

CUE: Keep the arm straight during the toss to develop consistency.

The racket is held behind the head in the "back-scratch" position (see figure 3.18). As the toss leaves the fingers, reach up for the ball as high as possible without jumping. Bring the weight forward onto the front foot and contact the ball at full extension of the arm. If the toss has been made correctly, the ball should be contacted just in front of and to the right of the front foot.

Full Serve

The full serve is a more fluid and complete motion than the beginner's serve. Because of this, there is much greater opportunity for speed to be generated. A powerful serve is intimidating to opponents, especially when it is combined with effective placement. A hard, well-placed serve puts the receiver on the defensive and often sets up the point for the server. Since winning points and games is the objective, a strong, consistent, accurate serve is one of the game's premier elements. A weak, inconsistent, or erratic serve is a signal to the opponent that the player is probably not one to be reckoned with. More to the point, a weak serve invites the opponent to attack it, leading to a defensive posture on the part of the server.

Figure 3.18
Beginner's serve

Starting position

Contact

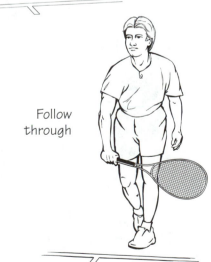

Follow through

slice

Unlike the beginner's serve, which uses the eastern forehand grip, players executing the full serve do so with the continental grip. The continental grip provides a flat surface for a square contact with the ball. For the continental grip, the V formed by the thumb and the fingers points to the left side of the wrist (for a right-handed player). To add spin to the serve, move the wrist a little more to the backhand side. Many players make even more of a grip adjustment to the backhand side in order to **slice** the second serve.

The stance for the full serve is similar to that described for the beginner's, or punch, serve. The front foot should be pointed toward the left net post and the body aligned in roughly a 45-degree angle toward the net. Both the toss arm and racket arm should start out in front of the body pointing toward the target (see figure 3.19). From that point on, however, the two arms take much different paths to accomplish a common goal. The toss arm, with the ball held between the thumb and fingers, is brought downward, then across the body, and finally up to shoulder level where it releases the ball. As described earlier, to the server, this motion simulates the letter J in the air. The racket is brought down past the right leg and up behind the back to the back-scratch position. From there the arm is extended to reach up and hit the ball.

To transfer the weight forward (an important source of power), bring the rear foot up to but not touching the baseline. By pushing with both feet and extending the knees, additional leverage may be achieved by reaching up to maximum height. Once contact is made with the ball, continue with the trail leg into the court. Follow through with the racket toward the target, then down and across the body.

CUE: Extend the legs to reach up for the ball.

Many players lack a consistent serve because they fail to spend the same amount of time practicing the serve as they do other strokes. The rhythmic motion needed to coordinate the action of the body's different movements must be repeated

Figure 3.19
Full serve.

a Continental grip   b Place ball up into position   c Move racket back   d Back scratch

often, as do the individual body movements. The toss alone requires special attention because it involves use of the nondominant hand. A good toss can make a world of difference, because when the toss is off, the racket arm must adjust the contact point. The result of a poor toss is a loss of power or accuracy or both. For this reason, players are well advised to develop the habit of catching the ball or letting it drop when the toss is off.

CUE: Develop a comfort zone for your toss. When you toss outside your comfort zone, let the ball drop and try again.

Slice Serve

"You're only as good as your second serve" is a commonly used phrase by coaches who try and impress upon players the value of an effective, reliable second serve. The slice serve is the most common type of second serve (see figure 3.20). It carries less pace but is easy to execute and can be hit with just as much effort as the first **flat serve.** Players who try to ease up during the second serve often find themselves double-faulting. With a slice serve, the player does not need to ease up at all. Players should adjust the grip, toss, and contact point with the ball, but not the effort. By keeping the effort level constant between first and second serves, you are less likely to double-fault. The grip is slightly shifted toward the backhand grip. The toss is further out to the side. The slicing action is made by striking the outside of the ball. Other stroke mechanics are the same as the full serve. Double faults due to an inconsistent second serve are easy points for the receiver. A good second serve can therefore win matches for the server.

Table 3.4 summarizes key elements and common errors in the serve.

flat serve

Figure 3.19
Continued.

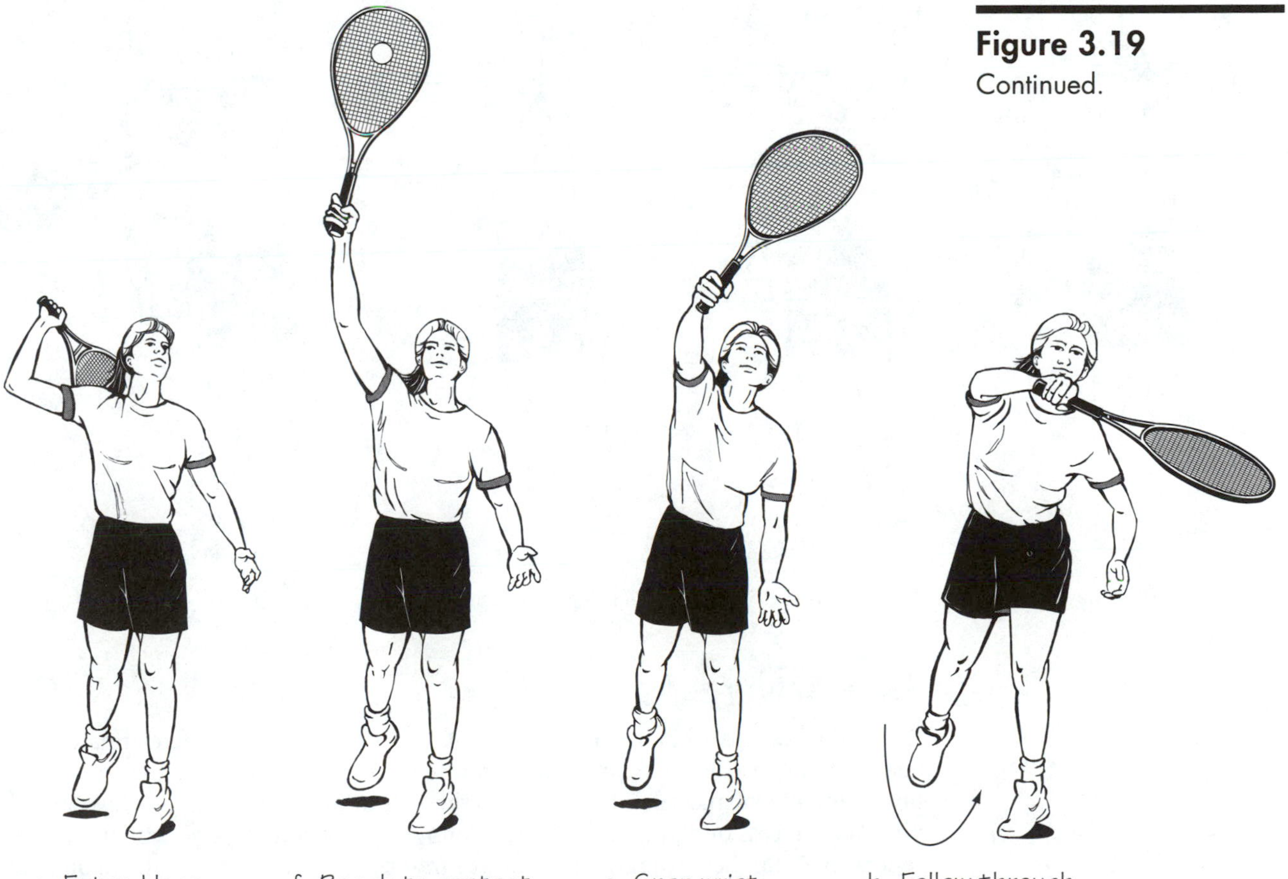

e Extend legs   f Reach to contact   g Snap wrist   h Follow through

Figure 3.20
Slice serve.

a Place ball into position

b place ball into up position

c Move racket back

d Back-scratch position

e Extend legs

f Contact

g Slice across ball

h Follow through across body

Serve Return

Returning serve is an important element of tennis that is often underestimated. For years, tennis teachers and coaches taught that the main purpose of the service return was to block the serve back to keep the ball in play. Although this is good advice, the success of players like Jimmy Connors and Andre Agassi, who developed reputations for being aggressive service returners, has changed this approach

TABLE 3.4	Key elements and common errors: The serve

READY PHASE	
Key Elements	**Common Errors**
1. Eastern or continental grip	1. Wrong grip
2. Stand sideways, facing net post	2. Body faces net
3. Put racket behind head for beginner serve; point racket arm and toss arm at target for full serve	3. No consistent starting position

EXECUTION PHASE	
Key Elements	**Common Errors**
1. Toss ball up and forward	1. Inconsistent ball toss, ball released too low or thrown into air
2. Move toss arm and racket arm upward together	2. Toss too low
3. Place ball into correct position	3. Serves go into net, ball drops too low before contact
4. Shift weight up and forward	
5. Reach high to contact ball	

FOLLOW-THROUGH PHASE	
Key Elements	**Common Errors**
1. Flex wrist at contact	1. No power in serve, lack of wrist flexion, leg extension, upper body rotation, or slow racket speed
2. Continue swing down and across	
3. Step forward into court after contact	

somewhat. Today, serve returners must be able to attack a weak serve as well as block back the tough ones.

Effective service return begins with observing the server's ball toss. By watching the toss carefully, you are trying to pick up any advance notice by the server as to where the ball may be going and how hard it will be struck or with what, if any, spin. This information is invaluable because it helps to determine your preparation, timing, and choice of return.

Armed with the knowledge you gained from observing the toss (some teachers call it "anticipation"), pivot quickly out of the ready position into a side-facing position. At the same time, move the racket back, then swing forward to punch through the ball (see figure 3.21). The amount of backswing and effort exerted in the forward swing determines to what extent the return is an aggressive one or a defensive one. Second serves (or weak first serves) are generally hit more aggressively with a longer backswing.

CUE: Return the ball about 3 to 4 feet above the net unless the server is approaching the net to volley. By hitting high over the net, you reduce the potential for hitting into the net and you put the ball deep into the opponent's court.

Figure 3.21
Serve return.

Backswing

Forward swing

Follow through

In spite of the time you will have to prepare for the service return, several circumstances will require last-second adjustments on your part. The wide variety of speeds, spins, and angles are just a few of these factors. Wind direction and velocity must also be accounted for when returning serve. Finally, whether the server rushes the net or stays back is vitally important to your choice of returns.

For hard-hitting servers, stand back of the baseline about a yard or so to give yourself more time to see the ball. A difficulty with this tactic is that the ball will often have bounced so high by the time it reaches you, that nothing more than a weak return is possible. An alternative, therefore, is to hit the ball on the rise, which is done by standing just inside the baseline and blocking or slicing the return. The backswing is shortened and there is very little time to see the ball, but you can sometimes time the shot so that the power of the serve is transferred back into the return.

If you find that the server is able to serve and volley against you, hit your returns crosscourt so that you don't have to chase sharply angled volleys. A crosscourt return may entice the server into hitting the volley down the line so that you don't have to run any wider than the sideline.

Serve and Return Drills

#21: Mirror Serve Drill

Players line up across the baseline and practice service technique including the grip, stance, toss, backswing, contact, and follow-through without the ball (see Figure 3.22). Variation: The racket cover can be left on for added resistance to strengthen the arm.

#22: Serve Toss Drill

Players stand behind the baseline and practice the toss motion (see figure 3.23). Emphasize the J motion with a straight arm and placing the ball into position. The ball should drop a few inches inside the baseline.

#23: Change of Distance Drill

Players serve from the service line using the beginner's serve (see figure 3.24). After several minutes, all players move back to halfway between the service line and baseline and serve again. Players then move back all the way to the baseline and serve once again. As you move farther back, also move your contact point with the ball above your head farther back.

#24: Serve to Target Drill

Place a target within the service court—for example, as shown in figure 3.25. Try hitting the target. For variation, several targets can be placed in various positions. Score a point for each target hit.

Figure 3.22
Mirror serve drill (a).

Figure 3.23
Serve toss drill (b).

Figure 3.24

Change of distance serve drill (a).

Figure 3.25

Serve to target drill (b).

a   b

Figure 3.26

Toss accuracy drill.

#25: Toss Accuracy Drill

Players stand with both feet shoulder-width apart and about an inch behind the baseline. The racket is placed down on the court with the handle edge just touching the inside of the baseline and the head of the racket pointing toward the net (see figure 3.26). Once this is done, assume the server's stance by pointing the front foot toward the right net post and positioning the back foot behind and parallel to the baseline. Using good technique, the player attempts to toss the ball as if for a serve, landing the ball on the racket strings. Count the number of successful tosses out of 10.

#26: Serve and Return Drill

One player serves balls at medium speed, which the receiver tries to return between 3 and 4 feet above the net so they land near the baseline. After 10 serves/returns, players switch roles.

#27: One, Two, and Over Drill

One player delivers a first serve, which is blocked back by the receiver. The server then serves a second serve, which is attacked by the receiver. The drill may be stopped after the return or the point is played out. After four points, the players switch roles and the drill is repeated.

#28: Five-Point Serve and Return Game

Two players play a game to 5 points using only serves and serve returns. The server gets two chances to successfully place a serve in the service court that cannot be returned past the service line by the receiver. Every good serve that is not returned past the service line counts as a point for the server. Every return that lands in the **backcourt** counts as a point for the receiver. Reverse roles after each game of 5 points.

SKILL 4 | Volley

The **volley** is a shot hit before the ball bounces. It is usually hit from the area between the service line and the net but could be played from the backcourt on occasion. Because the player is usually closer to the net, there is less time to prepare for the shot. The result is a shorter backswing and a grip that allows the player to volley the ball from either side without changing.

Volleys are designed as an offensive tactic to force the play to an early conclusion. In serve and volley tennis, the player serves, moves to the net, sets the ball up with a placement volley, then moves forward and puts the ball away with an aggressive volley.

Volleying the ball effectively requires good hand-eye coordination and well-practiced technique. The player should use the continental grip to hold the racket. The continental grip allows the player to punch the ball with a solid grip on both forehand and backhand sides (see figures 3.27 and 3.28). The continental grip is

volley

Figure 3.27
Forehand volley.

Ready position

Pivot and turn

Short backswing

Begin step across

Squeeze racket

Forward swing

Follow through

Figure 3.28
Backhand volley.

Ready position   Pivot and turn   Short backswing

Step across   Squeeze at contact   Follow through

basically the middle ground between the eastern forehand and backhand grips. The V formed by the thumb and fingers points to the center of the body when the racket is held in front of the body.

Hitting volleys involves a blocking or punching motion, which is accomplished by bringing the racket out to the side of the body but not much further back. This shortens the backswing, which is essential because of the proximity to the net and velocity of the oncoming shot. There is simply not enough time to take a full backswing. Once the racket is out to the side of the body, attention should be paid to pivoting on the foot to the side where the ball is to be played. For a forehand volley, the player should pivot on the right foot, then step across the body with the left foot. How far across the step should go depends on the position of the ball as it approaches. If time permits, the player should try to step toward the net and use the body's forward linear momentum to add power to the shot.

The swing itself is accomplished by keeping the racket head high while attacking the ball out in front and to the side of the body. The wrist should be kept firm throughout the swing, with the action of swinging initiated at the shoulder.

CUE: Keep the elbows up and out from the body. This will keep the racket out in front of the body and in a good position to volley.

The follow-through is an important component of the volley because it adds depth to the shot. Volleys should be played deep into the backcourt away from the opponent. Once played, the player should quickly resume the ready position at the net because of the high probability that the ball will be returned.

On many occasions, the player must make adjustments to volley technique in order to adapt to the many different circumstances that will occur. For low volleys, bend the knees to get down to the level of the ball. By bending the knees, you avoid having to volley up on the ball, a practice that allows your opponent to hit down on the return. For high volleys, accentuate the stiffness in the wrist and elbow, making sure the arm movement is initiated from the shoulder. When volleying a ball from at or behind the service line, it will be important to extend both the backswing and follow-through to generate enough force to place the ball deep into the backcourt.

CUE: Bend the knees for low volleys. Stiffen the arm for high volleys.

See table 3.5 for a summary of the key elements and common errors in the volley.

TABLE 3.5	Key elements and common errors: Volley
BACKSWING PHASE	
Key Elements	**Common Errors**
1. Continental grip	1. Incorrect grip
2. Short backswing	2. Backswing too long
3. Holds arms out from body with elbows near shoulder height	3. Stands too close or too far from net
FORWARD-SWING PHASE	
Key Elements	**Common Errors**
1. Step across with the front foot	1. Racket turns in the hand
2. Reach forward to meet the ball and tighten the grip	2. Ball is hit late
3. Bend to level of the ball	3. On backhand, elbow leads action
FOLLOW-THROUGH PHASE	
Key Elements	**Common Errors**
1. Little follow-through	1. Ball is hit down, not out
2. Watch opponent after shot	2. Lack of power

Figure 3.29
Mirror volley drill.

Figure 3.30
Copycat volley drill.

Figure 3.31
Toss and volley drill.

Drill and Self Test Volley Drills

#29: Mirror Volley Drill

Players line up across the court facing the net about halfway between the service line and the net. Players can be on both sides of the net. From the ready position, players practice volley technique including the grip, footwork, backswing, contact, follow-through, and return to ready position without the ball (see figure 3.29). Practice both forehand and backhand volleys.

#30: Copycat Volley Drill

Players pair up with one on each side of the net facing each other (see figure 3.30). From the ready position, one player begins the volley technique and the other attempts to copy the action to the same side without the ball. They repeat several times using high, low, wide, and close volleys, then switch roles.

#31: Toss and Volley Drill

Players pair up across the net from each other. The volleyer should stand 5 to 8 feet from the net. The tosser should stand on or near the service line (see figure 3.31). The ball is tossed to the side of the player at the net, who volleys it back to the tosser. Accuracy should be emphasized by trying to volley back into the hands of the tosser. After several successful volleys, players switch roles.

#32: Groundstroke to Volley Drill

One player stands at the baseline and the other is at the net (see figure 3.32). The ball can be hit from either player to start the drill. The player at the baseline tries to keep the ball in play by hitting the ball over the net so that the net player can volley it. The net player tries to volley the ball back with a solid contact so that the ball bounces just beyond the service line. After several successful exchanges, players switch positions.

#33: Move Forward to Volley Drill

One player stands at the baseline and the other is across the net at the service line. The player at the baseline feeds the ball across the net. The other player volleys the ball back to the baseline player, then moves a few feet toward the net. This sequence is repeated until the volleyer reaches the net position, wherein each player tries to win the point.

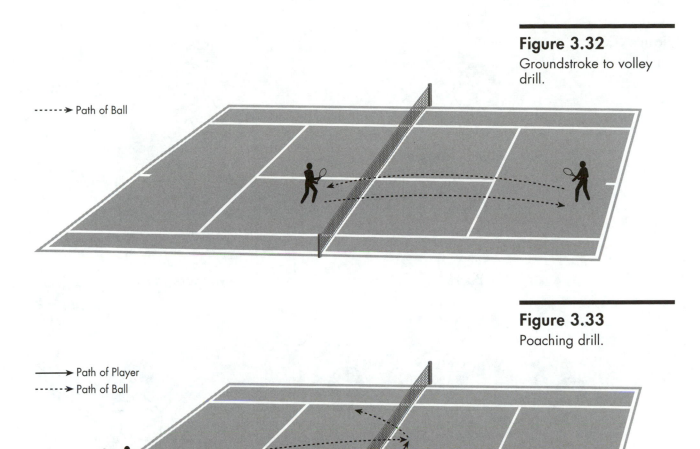

Figure 3.32
Groundstroke to volley drill.

- - - - - → Path of Ball

Figure 3.33
Poaching drill.

——→ Path of Player
- - - - - → Path of Ball

#34: Poaching Drill

One player is at the baseline and the other is at the net. The player at the net feeds a ball to the other player who returns it crosscourt (see figure 3.33). The player at the net waits until the baseline player's feet are planted, then moves across and volleys the ball into the open court. After the player performs the **poach** several times, the players switch roles.

poach

SKILL 5 | Lob

The **lob** is a shot played high and deep, often over the head of the opponent. The lob is used most often as a defensive ploy, to move the opponent away from the net or give the player time to recover from the opponent's pressure. Another type of lob, the **offensive lob,** on the other hand, is a high-risk, high-reward shot that often results in an outright winner if hit correctly.

Fundamentally, lobs are not much different from other groundstrokes. The swing trajectory starts in a low position and finishes high, although the amount of backswing is reduced (see figures 3.34 and 3.35). The amount of force imparted to the shot is, of course, substantially less than for other groundstrokes.

lob

offensive lob

Figure 3.34
Forehand defensive lob.

Backswing

Angle racket face

Swing low to high

Lift ball

Follow through

This is because the opponent's previous shot has usually been an offensive one, and little power is required to return it. Occasionally, the player may have only enough time to block the ball with an angled racket face to get it up and over the opponent.

CUE: Open the racket face and shorten the backswing.

The offensive lob is a much more difficult shot to execute but one that can be an effective alternative to a regular diet of passing shots. This shot can be hit with or without topspin. With a flat racket face, lift the ball upward just high enough to clear the opponent's outstretched racket. For the topspin offensive lob, try to accentuate the topspin imparted to the ball by increasing the tempo of the shot. Lobs should be played more often into the wind and to the opponent's backhand side.

Table 3.6 summarizes the key elements and common errors in the lob.

Figure 3.35
Backhand defensive lob.

Backswing

Open racket face

Swing low
to high

Lift ball

Follow through

TABLE 3.6	Key elements and common errors: Lob

BACKSWING PHASE	
Key Elements	**Common Errors**
1. Forehand grip	1. Too much or too little backswing
2. Short backswing	2. Worries about player at net and does not
3. Keep eyes focused on ball	focus on the ball

FORWARD-SWING PHASE	
Key Elements	**Common Errors**
1. Open racket face	1. Lob is too short or too deep
2. Lift ball up and over net player	

FOLLOW-THROUGH PHASE	
Key Elements	**Common Errors**
1. Finish swing high	1. No follow-through at target

Figure 3.36
Lob drill.

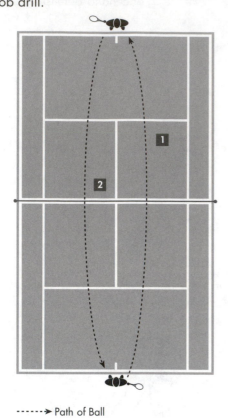

------▶ Path of Ball

Lob Drills

#35: Lob Drill

Players stand at their respective baselines and lob the ball back and forth across the net trying to keep the ball within the court boundaries for as long as possible (see figure 3.36).

#36: Volley and Lob Drill

One player stands at the net with the other at the baseline. The player at the net feeds a ball to the baseline player who lobs high and deep over the net player (see figure 3.37). The net player should reach up with the racket to allow the baseline player to gauge the lob angle and power to be used. After several successful lobs, switch roles.

#37: Continuous Lob and Smash Drill

With players in the volley and baseline positions, alternate controlled lobs and smashes back and forth for as long as possible (see figure 3.38). Repeat several times, then switch positions.

SKILL 6 Smash

The smash, or **overhead** as it is often called, is the most offensive shot in tennis. It may be hit from anywhere on the court but is most effective when used in the frontcourt. Any serve and volleyer must possess a good smash because of the high probability of the lob. A good overhead is very intimidating because it puts pressure on opponents to make perfect shots. It is also one of the few shots where you can hit all out, which can be both exhilarating to the player and demoralizing to the opponent.

Fundamentally, the overhead smash is executed with the continental grip. Once the player sees that the ball has been lobbed, the most important thing is to hurry into position early and wait for the ball to descend. The correct position is illustrated in figure 3.39. Take small steps to move the body behind and under the ball's anticipated descent. At the same time, bring the racket up behind the head into the back-scratch position. The toss arm should be raised to track the flight of the ball for greater accuracy in meeting the ball at the correct point.

Figure 3.37
Volley and lob drill.

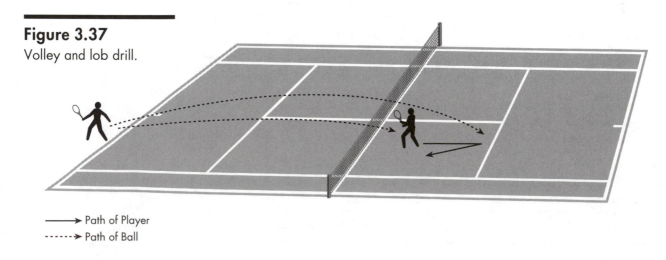

——▶ Path of Player
------▶ Path of Ball

Figure 3.38

Continuous lob and smash drill.

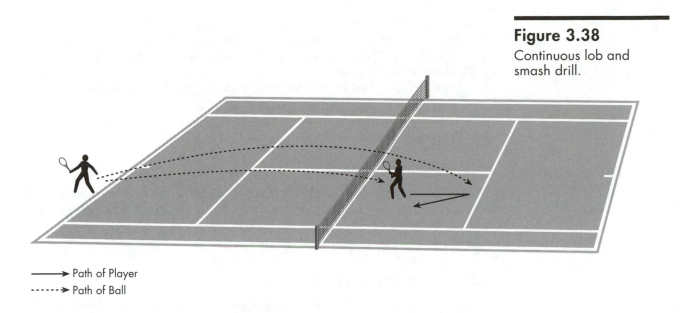

⟶ Path of Player

------→ Path of Ball

CUE: Hurry and wait for the overhead.

The smash itself is similar to the serve. From the back-scratch position, bring the racket forward and up to meet the ball as high as possible. As the arm and racket move forward to contact the ball, the weight should also move forward to generate force. At contact the wrist should be snapped forward and down to add more velocity and to keep the ball in the court. In the follow-through, the racket should go naturally down and across the body. Once finished, the player should return to the ready position for the return. In cases where there is not enough time

Figure 3.39

Overhead smash.

Footwork

Backswing

High contact

Follow through

to get into position, it may even be necessary to jump into the air and back before smashing. This, of course, eliminates the possibility of moving the weight forward into the shot. To compensate, the wrist snap should be accentuated to bring the ball down into the court.

See table 3.7 for the key elements and common errors in the overhead smash.

■ Overhead Smash Drills

#38: Mirror Smash Drill

Players line up across the court facing the net about halfway between the service line and the net. Players can be on both sides of the net. From the ready position, players practice smash technique, including the body turn, footwork, backswing, contact, follow-through, and return to ready position without the ball.

#39: Toss and Smash Drill

Players pair up across the net from each other. The player at the net should stand 5 to 8 feet from the net. The tosser should stand on or near the service line and to one side of the court (see figure 3.40). The ball is tossed up high to the player at the net, who smashes it. Emphasize accuracy by trying to smash to a specific zone. After several successful smashes, players switch roles.

TABLE 3.7   Key elements and common errors: Overhead smash

BACKSWING AND MOVEMENT PHASE	
Key Elements	**Common Errors**
1. Take short, quick steps to get into position under and behind ball	1. Fails to move the body into position
2. Put racket up behind head early	2. Racket late in moving up behind head
3. Turn body sideways to net	3. Wrong grip, player forgets to change to continental grip
4. Track ball with free arm	
5. Hurry into position and wait for ball	

FORWARD-SWING PHASE	
Key Elements	**Common Errors**
1. Start swing early	1. Ball drops too low before hitting
2. Reach up to contact ball high	2. Body is still moving while shot is being made
3. Shift weight forward into shot	

FOLLOW-THROUGH PHASE	
Key Elements	**Common Errors**
1. Follow-through at target	1. No racket speed generated on ball
2. Flex wrist on contact for power	2. Target changed at last second
3. Swing out, then down and across the body	

Figure 3.40
Toss and smash drill.

------→ Path of Ball

#40: Lob and Smash Drill

One player stands at the baseline and the other is at the net. The ball can be hit from either player to start the drill. The player at the baseline tries to keep the ball in play by lobbing the ball up over the net so that the net player can smash it (see figure 3.41). The net player tries to smash the ball back with a solid contact so that the ball can be played by the baseline player. After several successful exchanges, players switch positions.

SKILL 7 | Half Volley

The **half volley** is a shot hit immediately after the bounce. The half volley is similar in technique to a groundstroke although the backswing is usually shortened to increase the accuracy of the shot. In most cases, the half volley is a defensive

half volley

Figure 3.41
Lob and smash drill.

shot, hit because the player is out of position or because of a well-placed shot by the opponent. In serve and volley tennis, the player may serve and approach the net hoping to volley, only to have the opponent play a shot that will land at or near the player's feet. Players must therefore become adept at the half volley because when played deep, it allows players to remain in the offensively advantageous net position.

The fundamental aspects of the half volley involve turning the side to the net, bending the knees to get the head and eyes down closer to the point of contact with the ball, and shortening the backswing (see figure 3.42). Beginners often make the mistake of trying to lift the ball up over the net. By slightly opening the racket face and staying down on the ball, players can angle the shot just over the net so that it lands deep into the backcourt. The amount of follow-through depends on where in the court the half volley is played from and the speed of the oncoming shot. In most cases, follow-through is sacrificed for improved accuracy.

CUE: Shorten the backswing and bend the knees to half-volley.

Table 3.8 summarizes the key elements and common errors in the half volley.

Half-Volley Drills

#41: Line to Line Drill

Players stand just behind their respective service lines. They drop and hit the ball to start and aim the ball to land at the service line (see figure 3.43). Players are forced in this way to hit half volleys back over the net. Alternate hitting forehand and backhand half volleys.

#42: Side to Side Half Volleys

One player stands at the net and the other is at the service line (see figure 3.44). The player at the net starts the drill by feeding a short ball wide to the forehand, which the player at the service line runs and returns softly with a half volley. The net player volleys the return wide to the backhand, which the player runs down and returns as before. This pattern continues for a set number of returns or until the player misses a return.

Figure 3.42
Half volleys.

Forehand
half volley

Backhand
half volley

TABLE 3.8	Key elements and common errors: Half volley

BACKSWING PHASE	
Key Elements	**Common Errors**
1. Bend down to the ball	1. Lowers racket head but not body
2. Shorten backswing	2. Takes long backswing

FORWARD-SWING PHASE	
Key Elements	**Common Errors**
1. Reach forward to contact ball early	1. Waits too long before hitting ball
2. Swing through slightly upward trajectory	2. Angles racket face upward
3. Hold racket tightly	3. Overswings, ball travels high and out

FOLLOW-THROUGH PHASE	
Key Elements	**Common Errors**
1. Adjust based on pace of oncoming shot	1. Too much follow-through, ball travels out
2. Point racket at target	

Figure 3.43
Line to line drill.

- - - - - ▶ Path of Ball

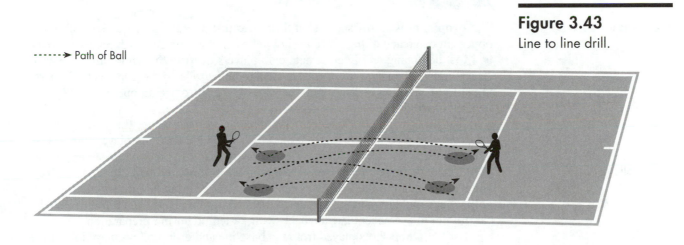

Figure 3.44
Side to side half volleys.

⎯⎯⎯▶ Path of Player
- - - - - ▶ Path of Ball

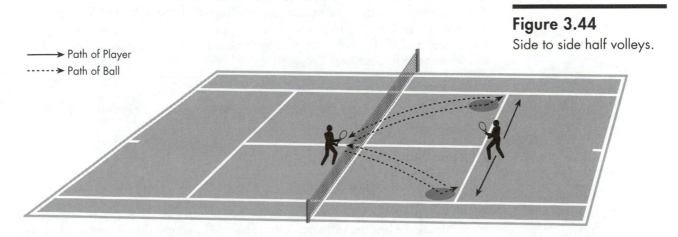

Figure 3.45
Half volley from no-man's land drill.

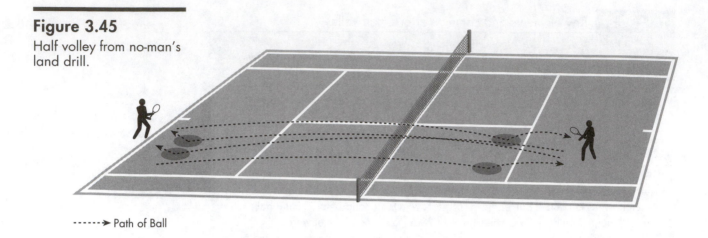

------→ Path of Ball

#43: Half Volley from No-Man's Land Drill

One player stands halfway between the service line and the baseline while the partner is across the net at the baseline (see figure 3.45). The players start a rally back and forth, playing half volleys from **no-man's land** back over the net. Players should try to hit their half volleys deep.

no-man's land

SKILL 8 Drop Shot

drop shot

The **drop shot** is an off-speed shot that lands just over the net and dies before the opponent can reach it. It is a pretty shot to be sure but difficult to execute effectively. Most beginning and intermediate club players overuse this shot. Since the drop shot is used primarily as a surprise tactical element to keep the opponent off guard, to exploit a weakness such as poor court mobility, or to tire an opponent, it should be used sparingly.

The fundamentals of the drop shot depend on from where the shot is played. Drop shots can be played from the baseline, in which case the player should disguise the shot by going through the same mechanical preparation as any other groundstroke. There should be no change in backswing, footwork, or tempo. **Drop volleys,** played from the frontcourt can also be played as an alternative to the punch volley but should look identical during the preparation phase. The player should be careful not to overaccentuate the backswing or tempo during preparation.

drop volley

For both drop shots played from the baseline and drop volleys played from the net, the racket face opens just before impact with the ball (see figure 3.46). The effect is like sliding a dish underneath, thus the common description of "dishing" the ball with the racket. This technique abbreviates the follow-through, which is an essential element of the drop shot. Adding backspin to the drop shot makes the ball die sooner after the bounce.

CUE: *Dish the racket under the ball on the drop shot.*

Table 3.9 summarizes the key elements and common errors in the drop shot.

Drop Shot Drills

#44: Drop Shot Option Drill

One player is at the net with the other at the baseline (see figure 3.47). To begin, one player drops and hits the ball to the other player. The player at the baseline attempts

Figure 3.46
Drop shot.

Backswing　　　　　Forward swing　　　　　Follow through

to hit a drop shot every few shots. The drop shot should be aimed to one side or the other just over the net. The player at the net should mix up shots to both forehand and backhand sides. After several successful drop shots, players reverse roles.

#45: Drop Shot Game

Play against your partner using only drop shots. Have the service line serve as the end line (see figure 3.48). Drop and hit to begin.

TABLE 3.9	Key elements and common errors: Drop shot
BACKSWING PHASE	
Key Elements	**Common Errors**
1. Same as groundstroke, disguise is important to success of shot	1. Grip is changed
FORWARD-SWING PHASE	
Key Elements	**Common Errors**
1. Open racket face	1. Angle of racket face too open
2. Swing from high to low	2. Used when too far from net
FOLLOW-THROUGH PHASE	
Key Elements	**Common Errors**
1. Stop swing sharply after contact	1. Too much follow-through

Figure 3.47
Drop shot option drill.

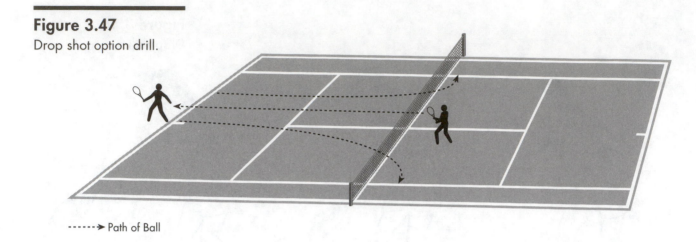

------▶ Path of Ball

Figure 3.48
Drop shot game.

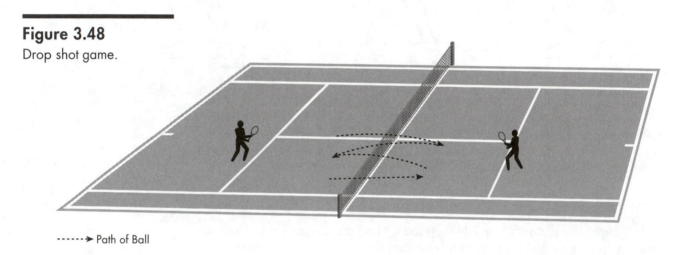

------▶ Path of Ball

Strategies

Concentration

Concentration is a psychological skill that can aid performance. Learning to concentrate takes time and practice and should be worked on in practice sessions as well during matches. Lapses in concentration due to on-court distractions often mean the difference between winning and losing. By practicing your concentration as well as your tennis skills, you should find that your ability to maintain concentration during a match improves.

In tennis, many distractions must be avoided if the player is to perform well. Concentrating means filtering out the irrelevant cues in the environment so that total focus can be paid to the relevant ones.

What are the relevant cues in tennis? Certainly watching the ball is a relevant cue. Some players worry more about what the other player is doing and lose concentration in the process. Another relevant cue is what many coaches call anticipation. Anticipation is really just focusing on the opponent to pick up any information that can tip off the kind of shot that will be played, the side of the court the ball will be hit to, what kind of spin is on the ball, and so on. Some players always seem to be in the right place at the right time; it appears they never have to run for the ball. That situation may result because the player is adept at focusing on cues given by the opponent at the time the ball is hit or before the ball is hit.

Another relevant cue is the ability to recognize game situations and to sort out the single most important variable to be considered when reacting to them. For example, when running wide to hit a groundstroke, there are probably a hundred things you could be thinking about at that moment. A few of the more common ones include the score at the time, whether or not you won the last point, how tired you feel, or whether you think you can reach the ball. Even if we could think of the ten to fifteen relevant cues for hitting a running forehand at that moment (not to mention the irrelevant ones), doing so would create what sports psychologists call "paralysis by analysis." In a laypersons's terms, it means thinking of too many things at once. The usual effect of paralysis by analysis is an error. The key is to find a particularly important factor and focus totally on it. In this example, it may be hitting the ball crosscourt because you know that your opponent is likely to be looking for a down-the-line return.

Irrelevant cues are merely distractions that compete for our attention but serve no useful purpose. The crowd noise, previously missed shots, perhaps even the score of the match fall into this category. Many coaches argue that even the technical elements of the skill being performed are also irrelevant at that moment and should not be attended to. They believe, as many sports psychologists do, that cognitive attention paid to a psychomotor function may interfere with execution of the skill. Although this may sound like psychological mumbo-jumbo to some, keep in mind that many successful tennis professionals try to think about absolutely nothing on the court. In other words, because they have developed the necessary neuromuscular pathways through endless practice, the players simply let their psychomotor skills take over and "flow."

Our normal attention span is limited to just a few seconds. Because a tennis match can last up to two hours or more, we must condition our minds to maintain longer periods of concentration. Bjorn Borg, one of the greatest tennis players of all time and master of intense concentration on the tour, remarked, "Very often in a tennis match, you can point to just one game where for a couple of points you lost concentration and didn't do the right thing, and the difference in the match will be right there." Learning to maintain concentration takes time as well as readiness on the part of the learner. Most players do not have a problem concentrating during points. It is between points that concentration lapses are common. Most rallies average 10 seconds in length with about 30 seconds taken between points. This means that in a 2-hour match, only 40 minutes or so are spent in actual play. The remaining 1 hour and 20 minutes represent opportunities where concentration may suffer. How might this time be used to maintain concentration?

Most successful tennis players will use some method of maintaining concentration. Even John McEnroe, whose emotional tirades on the court were legendary, was a master at concentrating when it counted. Many opponents seemingly crumbled after one of John's outbursts, but John himself rarely let his emotions affect his play. He was able to regain his concentration almost immediately. Here are some of the more common methods of developing concentration.

- Develop a routine. Routines are familiar and familiarity is reassuring in times of stress. Go through a particular ritual of preparing to serve or return serve and concentrate on it. Never vary the routine.
- Never change your mind on a shot. By changing your mind on a shot you begin to second-guess yourself and your strategy. Most times, changing the shot results in an error anyway, and the situation can develop into a vicious circle that ends in defeat.
- Use cue words. Cue words have several useful purposes, not the least of which is to act as an emotional stabilizer. Much like a "mantra" helps to force unwanted thoughts from the mind of the meditator, saying a cue word over and over to yourself helps to force negative thoughts out of the mind.
- Keep the eyes from wandering. Looking down at the court between points keeps the eyes from scanning the environment for irrelevant stimuli. If the eyes start to wander, the mind may not be far behind.
- Play one point at a time. Every tennis player understands how difficult this can be at times. Bjorn Borg was once asked to describe what he felt was his greatest attribute. He stated, "It was my ability to play one point at a time and not worry about and think about what just happened or what might happen." Even Borg had to learn this valuable skill the hard way. As a junior, his parents felt compelled to put his tennis racket in the closet for six months because his temper on the court got so bad. He obviously learned his lesson. Stay in the present and try not to dwell on the past or future.

Imagery

Imagine yourself sitting in your easy chair rehearsing in your mind how you will hit a powerful serve, then advance quickly to the net for a put-away volley of the service return. This scenario is an example of how the psychological skill known as imagery may be used. We imagine all kinds of things in everyday life, so why not in sports? Imagery is often referred to as mental practice, visualization, or mental rehearsal. Regardless of the name, the essence of imagery is creating or re-creating an experience in the mind (Robert S. Weinberg, The Mental Advantage [Champaign, IL: Leisure Press, 1988], p. 100). It's like physical practice except that the practice is going on inside your head. You use imagery every time you watch a top player and try to copy his or her strokes. You use imagery each time you think of how to play a certain point or the strategy you will use against an opponent. You use imagery each time you think of a situation that you know will occur in a match and how you will react to it.

Imagery is more than just visual in nature. It involves other senses as well, some or all of which may combine to produce the most complete image possible. Visual senses are used when you visualize the serving motion in your mind. See yourself placing the ball carefully into the air. See your legs extend upward. See your racket attack the ball. See the ball land where you want it to for an ace. Kinesthetic senses are used when you recall how it feels to contact the ball at the height of the toss with your weight moving upward and forward. How does your body feel to stretch up for the ball. How does your wrist feel as it snaps to bring the ball down into the court? Auditory senses are used when you recall the sound the ball makes as it comes off the strings when hit just right. Tactile sense is used when you feel how the racket feels in your hand.

Imagery training works because even though the body is not physically moving during the mental activity, the neuromuscular system is. If you were to mentally practice your serve, for example, your neural pathways that control your muscles would be strengthened. By imagining the perfect service motion, the body will actually believe it is practicing the serve, and the muscles related to serving will become programmed. If this sounds like it's too good to be true, try it and see. Watch a good tennis player serve, then mentally rehearse in your mind what you have seen. Then give it the acid test on the court.

There is another way in which imagery training can be helpful, which has to do with controlling one's emotions. Most tennis players experience various emotions at one time or another on the court. Having to deal with pressure, becoming angry, losing confidence, or feeling a sense of helplessness are some of these common experiences. Imagery training involves thinking of situations where these emotions are likely to surface, such as double-faulting on set point, missing an easy put-away, or making unforced errors. When re-creating the situation, try and notice the emotional effects that accompany it. Substitute a healthier alternative such as an element of concentration discussed in the previous section or one of the stress management techniques discussed next. Here are some ways in which imagery may be utilized:

- Go over the strokes in your mind. Practicing the strokes in your mind helps you to understand how all the elements fit together.
- Correct stroking errors. Mental imagery is a valuable tool in improving problem strokes.
- Review your performances to correct errors. Replaying the match in your mind to determine why you played a certain shot can be helpful in learning what decisions are made in certain situations. If those decisions result in frequent errors, corrections should be made.

- Develop new options. If your game plan has become somewhat predictable, spend some time thinking about other shots that could be played in particular situations. This may help to keep opponents off guard.
- Rehearse your game plan. Think about who you will be playing and what shots will give you trouble. Plan how you will deal with those situations.
- Plan some confidence-building images for problem situations. When you lose your service game, imagine yourself breaking back in the next game.
- Develop an image of yourself regaining your concentration when you encounter a situation where it lapses.
- Develop an image of yourself dealing with discomfort such as fatigue, pain, or hot weather (e.g., skiing in the mountains).

Stress Management

Coaches often tell their players to give 100 percent when playing. Giving 100 percent on the tennis court, however, can spell disaster. Tension created in the muscles, such as when you try and hit the ball as hard as possible, interferes with the body's already developed neuromuscular patterns. The result is usually a weaker shot or lost accuracy. The act of hitting a tennis ball with more velocity actually requires less tension in the muscles that work against the muscles needed to perform the movement so that the racket head speed can be increased. Think about giving 80 percent or 90 percent effort instead of 100 percent. Experienced tennis players have a learned sense that is able to detect extra tension when it appears and can make the necessary adjustments. Tension can be released by several methods.

One of the most utilized relaxation techniques is progressive relaxation. In this method, you progress from one muscle group to the next, alternately tensing and relaxing the muscles. This method teaches you to recognize muscle tension when it is experienced and how to release it. If you have a habit of getting nervous the day of a match, you could try progressive relaxation beforehand.

Progressive relaxation should be done in a quiet, dimly lit room where you can lie down. Remove or loosen any tight clothing. Close your eyes, take a deep breath and begin tensing and relaxing the muscles, one muscle group at a time. With practice, progressive relaxation can be done on cue, a skill that may prove useful when in the midst of a pressure-packed match.

On the court, there are several useful methods of managing stress:

- Relax your jaws when you feel tension in the body.
- Between points, take a few deep breaths to relax the neck and shoulders.
- Instead of holding your breath with every shot, breathe out with each hit. Some players, like Monica Seles, emit a grunt with each shot. Breathing out releases tension in the muscles.
- Frequently shake out the tension in the neck, shoulders, and hands.
- Tell yourself to relax. Verbalizing is the mind's way of triggering the relaxation response. Of course, this will only be effective if you have mastered your relaxation skills.
- Unclutter your mind. Trying to process too much information all at the same time often leads to increased tension. If you focus on one thing at a time, not only will you be able to manage your stress level but your concentration will also improve.
- Stay in the present. Worrying about a prior bad shot or what might happen if you double-fault increases anxiety and muscle tension, which often results in more mistakes. If you worry about choking, chances are you will.

- Go for it on the court. The feeling you get after playing your best is an unmistakable one. You feel unbeatable, ready to take on all comers. If you were to analyze the tension in your muscles during this state, you would likely find it to be very low. In other words, when you are playing well, you are relaxed on the court. During these times, you tend to go for your shots and not worry about the consequences. It doesn't mean hitting all out on every shot or going for a winner every time. It does mean taking advantage of opportunities to pressure your opponent. If you are afraid to make a mistake and play tentatively as a result, you will never know just how good you can play.

- Have fun out there. Why would anyone play a sport and not want to enjoy themselves while playing? Players who play but do not enjoy the game probably have extrinsic incentives such as prizes or prestige as their main motivation. Certainly winning is fun, but you can't win every time. Nor should it be the main focus if you want to truly enjoy the game. Remember that when you first started playing a sport, the fun was playing the game. As players improve, the fun part of the game sometimes gets supplanted by other pressures such as winning or pleasing parents or coaches. This is one reason that many players drop out of competitive sports—a sad indictment of American sport to be sure, but one we can do something about if we put the emphasis back where it belongs, and that is to have fun.

Self-Talk

Self-talk occurs anytime you think about something, not just when the words are verbalized. The next time you watch a tennis match, notice how the players talk to themselves. For one thing, you will see a wide variety of emotions being expressed—discouragement, anger, hopelessness, optimism, elation. How many of these emotions are evident even when no words are spoken? Clearly, you will note that there is both negative and positive self-talk. Negative self-talk is irrational or tension-producing and detracts from performance. Conversely, positive self-talk helps players stay focused on the present and not dwell on past mistakes.

Sport scientists have determined that peak performance occurs when players do not think about what they are doing. Most tennis players do think before and after each point, however, and this makes the ability to control these thoughts most important.

As just noted, some thoughts can be destructive. Double-faulting in tennis is a fairly regular occurrence and one that lends itself to negative self-talk. Although it is difficult to be positive in this situation, it is important to your future play to stop the negative self-talk and substitute positive thoughts. Try substituting some cue words for the negative emotions you may be feeling. Instead of, "I choked. If I do that again, I'll never win this match," try, "let's calm down and take it one point at a time. Just concentrate on the toss and everything will be fine." Several other circumstances that can lead to negative self-talk include blowing a big lead, having your serve broken, making unforced errors, or missing an easy shot. Watch for these circumstances and your reactions to them. Can you substitute healthy cue words for the negative emotions you may be feeling?

Self-talk can be useful in other ways. Here are a few of them that can be incorporated into your game plan:

- Use some cue words to help get you motivated if you are sluggish in your play. The words can be specific to the shot being played. For example, each time you go back to serve, say *explode* or *reach* to yourself. For a volley, say *punch* or *strong*. Cue words such as *move it* or *get going* can also help you become more energetic on the court.

- Use self-talk to remind yourself of important technical cues when learning new strokes. Reminding yourself to keep the *wrist firm* or the *knees bent* can be achieved through self-talk just before the stroke is executed. As proficiency increases, the cues should reflect more strategic elements of the game, such as where to hit the serve instead of how to hit it.

- When changing certain undesirable elements of your game, highlight the technical aspect needed instead of the mistake. For example, if you need more follow-through on your backhand, tell yourself to follow through instead of berating yourself for not doing so. The desired response will become more a part of your game, and you won't tense up in the process.

- When you find yourself lapsing into negative self-talk, try to substitute positive thoughts instead. We can't eliminate all negative self-talk from our minds, but we can learn to recognize and cope with it when it occurs. Once again, most of us are familiar with those situations on the court that lead to negative self-talk. When you notice negative thoughts creeping into your mind, stop them abruptly. This may be difficult to do at first, but it will get easier with practice. Taking a deep breath as you substitute a positive cue word will help to relax you as well.

- Be realistic about your capabilities. If you expect to play a perfect match, you will be disappointed. Realize that you will make errors but that these can be kept to a minimum by using the aforementioned psychological skills. Realize, too, that you have a reasonable amount of control over how you play. If you blame everything and everyone around you for your poor performance, you will become known as a poor sport. Likewise, if you start off poorly in a match, ranting about it will usually make things worse. Accept the past and try to improve the future.

- Remember, it's only a game. In the grand scheme of things, whether you win or lose a tennis match is not that important. It is not a reflection of your worth as a person, nor should you let it affect the rest of your life. Be thankful you have enough health and vigor to play the game.

GAME/ACTIVITY STRATEGIES

Singles Play

There are two general styles of play in singles. The baseline style of tennis requires penetrating groundstrokes, quickness, endurance, consistency, and the patience to keep the ball in play as long as it takes to force an error from the opponent. The baseliner relies on good groundstrokes and the ability to chase down most shots.

The serve and volley style of tennis requires a strong serve, accurate volley, good court movement, and powerful smash. Points are won or lost quickly, with one player usually at the net. The server rushes the net after each serve, hoping to elicit a weak return to be volleyed and eventually hit away for a winner.

Although most players prefer to play one style of tennis or the other, sooner or later, the baseline player will play an opponent who is so steady from the baseline that changing to a serve and volley style of play is an effective strategy. Of course, a change in strategy is only effective if the player can execute the skills. This means that players should spend time practicing both the serve and volley and baseline styles of tennis.

The Baseline Game

Groundstrokes are the foundation of this style of play. At the beginning level, the ability to keep the ball in play may be enough to provide success. Beyond this, however, a baseliner must develop powerful, penetrating groundstrokes that set up winners. This important element, combined with a few tactical points, will help to build a formidable baseline style of play:

- Hit most groundstrokes deep. This keeps opponents in the backcourt away from the net.
- Hit most groundstrokes crosscourt. The net is lower at the center than at the sidelines, which allows more margin for error on shots. It also changes the shape of the court from a rectangle to a diamond, which adds distance from corner to corner. A running groundstroke that pulls you out of the court should almost always be played high over the net and crosscourt because it will take longer to land, giving you more time to recover for the return.
- Return to home base after each shot. Home base is just behind the baseline in the center of the court. Begin to move back to home base after your shot.
- Shade the court slightly. Shading the court is done to encourage opponents to hit the ball to your stronger side (see figure 4.1). If your forehand is much stronger than your backhand, shade the court by standing slightly to the backhand side of the center mark. Be careful not to shade too far or you may find yourself hitting on the run. Also, some players like to run around the backhand, which, although effective in some situations, may pull you out of the court for the return.
- Be steady and get the ball back. Most points are won on errors, not winners. There is no point in playing baseline tennis if you can't keep the ball in play. Be patient and wait for the weak return to attack.
- Find your opponent's weaker stroke and exploit it. For most players this is the backhand. Try not to be fooled by a powerful but erratic shot. Tennis is still a game of percentages. Try to calculate which side, forehand or backhand, is weaker, then play mostly to that side, especially when you're on the defensive.
- Aim lower over the net and hit harder when the opponent is approaching the net. Although your margin for error is reduced, hitting lower makes the opponent play the ball with an open racket face. This creates an upward return that is easier to handle. Hitting harder makes the opponent play the ball from farther back, decreasing the changes of an offensive shot. Avoid hitting all out, however. More points are won on **passing shot** errors than volley winners, which suggests you should make your opponent beat you with the volley.
- Pass down the line or low crosscourt but never high crosscourt (see figure 4.2). Most passing shots should be hit down the line. Aim for a little inside the singles sideline. Another option is to hit the ball crosscourt but low over the net. The target here is where the service and singles sidelines meet. A third option is to lob over the head of the player at the net. The lob should be used whenever in trouble or for hard to handle shots.

passing shot

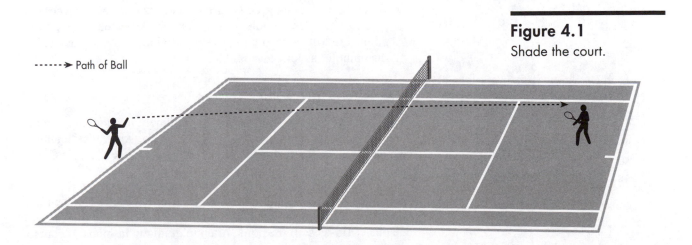

----→ Path of Ball

Figure 4.1
Shade the court.

Figure 4.2

Passing shot options.

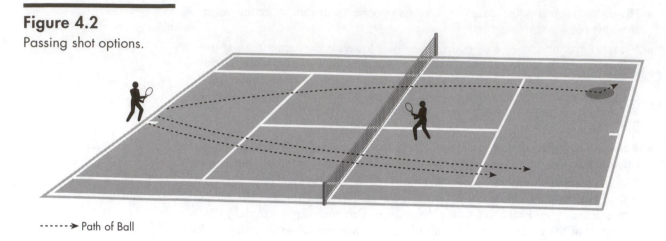

------> Path of Ball

- Occasionally vary the pace, spin, and placement of the ball. Changing these variables every so often prevents the opponent from becoming "grooved" on your groundstrokes. It also keeps the opponent guessing as to what kind of return is coming.

- Block back hard first serves, attack weak second serves. This strategy puts pressure on the server, who knows that any missed first serve will result in being put on the defensive. The server also knows that the first serves that are good will not result in easy points.

  - Bring in an opponent who doesn't like the net. One effective strategy for playing an opponent who likes to rally from the baseline is to force an approach to the net by taking some pace off the ball on the groundstroke. This makes the opponent play your game and puts him or her in an uncomfortable position at the net. Being in an uncomfortable position usually results in a defensive shot, giving you the option of passing or lobbing for the point.

  - Keep a serve and volleyer back by keeping shots high over the net and deep. It is better to sacrifice a little power for accuracy when you know the opponent is anxious to come to the net.

  - During a long rally from the baseline, show a pattern, then break it. The element of surprise is a valuable weapon. Set a pattern of hitting successive shots to one location, then change the pattern when it is least expected (see figure 4.3). Different patterns include the type of spin and pace as well as location of the shot.

  - When you're running down a ball and chances of a successful passing shot seem remote, throw up a lob. As stated earlier, more points are lost on errors than won on winners. Keep yourself in the point for as long as possible.

Figure 4.3

Show a pattern and break it.

------> Path of Ball

The Serve and Volley Game

Playing the game at the net can be an extremely invigorating experience for the serve and volley style player. Serve and volley tennis is characterized by the two elements denoting its name. A typical scenario for the serve and volleyer is a strong serve followed by a well-placed volley, then a put-away volley. In terms of strategy, the serve and volley style of tennis is much like a chess match. One player makes a tactical move, the other counters, and play continues until one player finishes off the point, often in dramatic fashion. Of course, the physical ability of the player is often what makes the serve and volley style of tennis so appealing. Good serve and volleyers must have a strong serve, accurate volley, powerful smash, and good footwork. Many would-be serve and volley style players do not possess superior physical strength and power, yet can develop a good serve and volley game through practice and the use of tactical maneuvers. The following is a list of tactical points to help serve and volley practitioners:

- Serve no more than 2 or 3 feet from the center mark. Any further puts you too far from the middle of the court, which is your target area.
- Toss the ball high and forward so that your weight transfer swings your trail foot into the court, becoming, in the process, the first step toward the net. Continue running to the net until the receiver hits the return, at which time you make a split-step stop; then adjust your court positioning to move to reach the return. In most cases, you will be near the service line when you make the first volley.
- Don't try to hit a service ace every time. Hitting aces takes a great deal of energy. Make sure you go for the aces at least once or twice each service game, but it may be more important to spot the serve to exploit an opponent's weakness.
- Serve mostly to the backhand side. The weakest return of serve for most players is the backhand, although you should test each player to confirm this. For every five serves you deliver, a good plan is to serve three to the backhand, one to the forehand, and one down the middle at the opponent's body. You can increase your ability to serve to the backhand side by standing further from the center mark when serving from the **ad court.** In the deuce court, the more powerful the serve, the farther the server should stand from the center mark (see figure 4.4).
- You're only as good as your second serve. Unless your first serve percentage is above 90 percent, you will need to have a good, dependable second serve. The second serve is not hit with as much pace as the first, but there is no reason why it can't be hit with just as much effort. By adjusting the grip on the racket, the toss, and the contact point with the ball, just as much energy can be exerted into the second serve, which adds spin and helps the ball cross higher over the net. The result is fewer double faults than if you hit the ball using less effort.
- Vary the spin and pace on the ball as well as placement. You want to avoid letting the opponent get into a service return groove. Keep him or her guessing about what serve is coming next. If you find one type that works over and over on an opponent, use it often.

ad court

Figure 4.4
Where to stand for the serve.

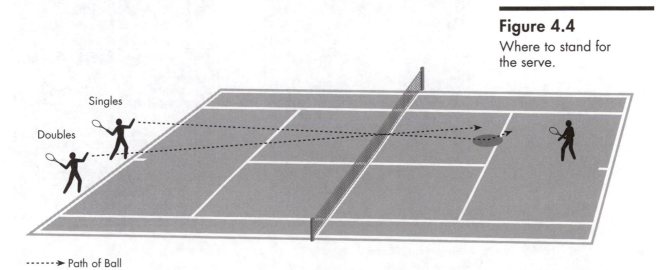

Singles

Doubles

- - - - - -▶ Path of Ball

- Decide your serve and volley strategy before each serve. The odds are in your favor if you serve wide because it pulls the opponent off the court, leaving an open court for the volley. Be stingy, however, about serving wide to the opponent's forehand because this is usually his or her stronger side. If your plan is to approach the net on the second serve, few, if any, serves should go to the opponent's stronger side.

- If your second serve is getting attacked, try adding depth and spin to it. Also, it's good strategy in such circumstances not to approach the net right away after the serve. Wait for a short ball and then make a good, deep approach shot, followed by movement to the net and, hopefully, a put-away volley.

- Hit most volleys deep into the open court. Deep shots keep the opponent at the baseline where there is less chance of being passed. Hitting the ball into the open court forces the opponent to run for your shot.

- Return a crosscourt shot down the line. Aim for the open space (see figure 4.5).

- Return a down-the-line shot crosscourt. Once again, the best angle for the volley is to the open area.

- Occasionally volley the ball behind the opponent. Once you've established a pattern of volleying the ball to the open area, wait for the opponent to start moving in that direction and then volley to the spot just vacated. This will wrong-foot the opponent and lead to future indecision as to where the ball will be played.

- Close on the net after the first volley. The first volley is usually played from near the service line and should therefore be considered more of a tactical shot than a put-away volley. By placing the ball deep into the open area, the player can move closer to the net and hit the return for a winner.

Figure 4.5

Crosscourt and down-the-line volleys.

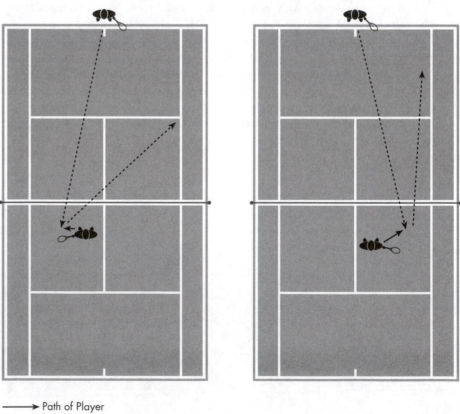

——→ Path of Player

------→ Path of Ball

Doubles Play

The objective of doubles play is to gain an offensive position at the net and win the point from that position. Because both teams have identical strategies, the successful team is the one that can play the most appropriate shot in the given situation to allow the team to advance. Whereas it may seem to the casual spectator that doubles is simply a matter of powerful serves, volleys, and smashes, tactics in doubles play a much larger role in the game than they do in singles. That is not to say that powerful shots are not important in doubles; they most certainly are. The advantage in each game is held by the serving team, of course, because of the strength of the serve. However, a well-placed return of serve can immediately turn the advantage to the receiving team. It is therefore necessary to learn the game of doubles from a tactical point of view as well as a technical one. Some suggestions are offered next.

Service Strategy in Doubles

- Stand farther from the center mark when serving in doubles in order to force the receiver into a wider position for the return. The wider position leaves more open court for your team's next shot.

- As a server, it is important for you to be able to spot the ball in specific locations because of your partner's position at the net. The net player should stand about 6 to 10 feet from the net (as shown in figure 4.6). Any weak return of serve because of a well-placed serve should be put away by the net player.

- Serve more often to the weaker stroke, usually the backhand. Because returns from the backhand are generally weaker, it is good strategy to serve to this side until the player proves to you that it is the stronger stroke.

- Come into the net position after every first serve and some second serves. The value of the serve (if returned) may be lost if the server does not move into the net position behind the serve. This is almost always the rule on the first serve. It can also be executed on the second serve if the serve is hit with spin to the receiver's weak side. By taking the net position, the opposition must hit a winning passing shot or lob, neither shot an easy prospect.

- Serve the ball wide to the forehand occasionally (see figure 4.7) and often to the backhand side in the ad court. Running the opponent out of the court to play a return is good strategy when there is a net player to hit the return. The net player should respect the possibility of a down-the-line return in this situation by taking a step toward the alley as the return is made.

- Start your serve with the stronger server. The order of serving can be changed at the beginning of each set, which means that you should start each set with your strength. If both players are about equal, consider the sun's position, wind direction, and who is playing well that day.

- Keep your partner in the game by serving down the middle (see figure 4.8). This is especially important if the net player is an effective volleyer or poacher. Serves down the middle offer less angle for the return. This allows the net player more opportunities.

- Spin the second serve in. This is done to gain more time to get to the net. If the receiver is hitting effective returns on your second serve, adjust the placement of your toss or your wrist position, to change the position of your racket as it contacts the ball. This may give you more depth on the serve. Another alterna-

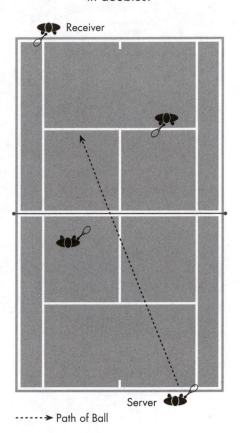

Figure 4.6

Starting positions in doubles.

Receiver

Server

- - - - -▶ Path of Ball

Figure 4.7
Wide doubles serve (a).

Figure 4.8
Down-the-middle doubles serve (b).

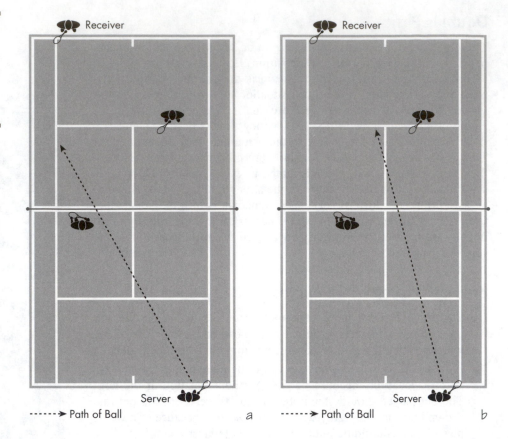

Receiver

Server

------▶ Path of Ball   a

Receiver

Server

------▶ Path of Ball   b

tive is to stay back after the serve and wait for a weak return, then hit an approach shot and come in to the net.

■ When playing a team that returns crosscourt effectively, consider switching to the Australian formation (see figure 4.9). In this formation, the server's partner starts at the net on the same side as the server. As the ball is served, the net player is in position to cover the crosscourt return. The server must therefore move to cover the down-the-line return. In the Australian formation there is usually more poaching than in traditional doubles. Many teams will use hand signals or short conferences after each point to plan their poaching strategy.

Serve Return Strategy in Doubles

■ Line up to cover the angle created by the server. As the server moves farther out toward the sideline to serve, you should also move wider and start your return of serve from there (see figure 4.10).

■ Move up for second serves and weaker servers (see figure 4.11). Remember, the strategy is to get to the net. If that can be accomplished with a good return of serve, then you will be closer to the net after the return. Standing inside the baseline also puts more pressure on the server to make the serve good.

■ Return serves to the feet of the server who comes in to the net, then come into the net (see figure 4.12). This return is executed with a low, flat crosscourt shot just over the net. This type of return forces the server to volley the ball upward, which gives your team the opportunity to reply with a downward shot.

■ Push the server wide with a sharply angled return to the alley. This return is a difficult one for the server to reach and usually results in the advantage being lost by the serving team.

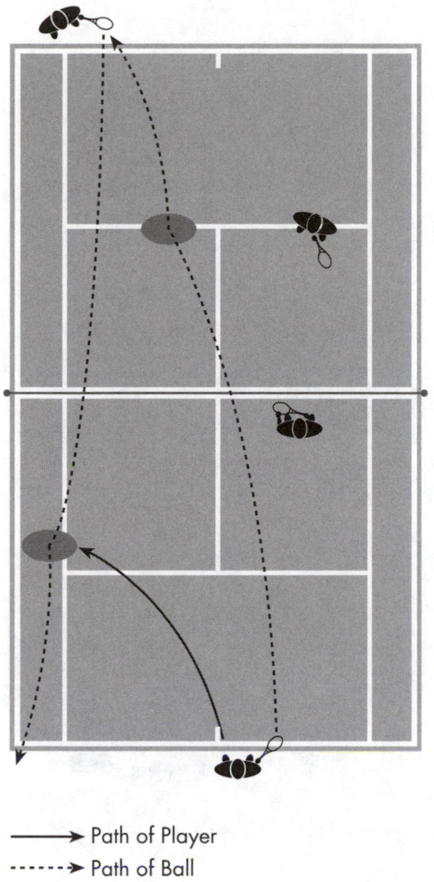

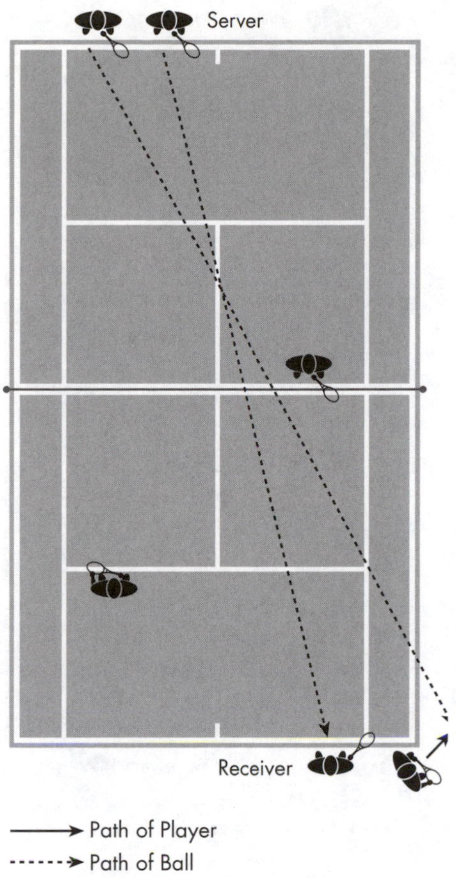

→ Path of Player
----→ Path of Ball

→ Path of Player
----→ Path of Ball

Figure 4.9 (on left)
Australian doubles formation.

Figure 4.10 (on right)
Server and receiver angles.

- Return the ball deep crosscourt when the server stays back, then come in to the net (see figure 4.13). By staying back, the server has allowed the other team to take the net position, and you should use the opportunity.

- If the server serves to your payoff stroke, make him or her pay. Hitting a wining return of serve early in a match can be a big boost because the server often makes a mental note never to come back to that side. This allows you to anticipate the serve coming to one side.

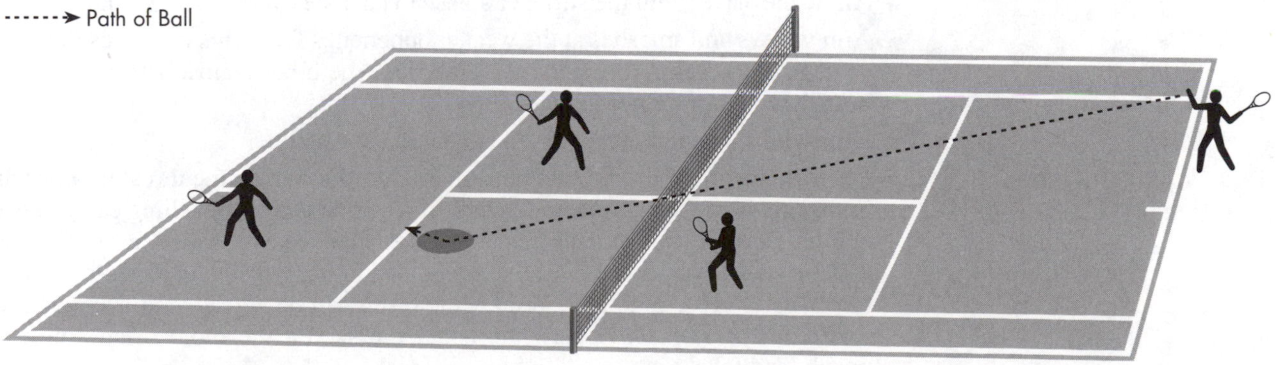

----→ Path of Ball

Figure 4.11
Receiver's position for second serve.

Figure 4.12
Return at server's feet (a).

Figure 4.13
Deep return and move
to net (b).

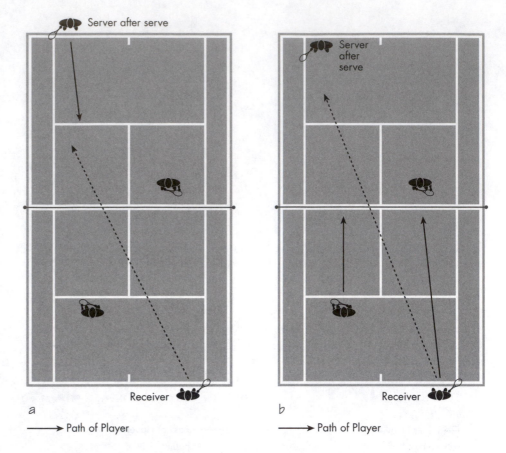

- If your partner (the receiver) has a strong return of serve, or the server has a weak serve, move up to the net position. This puts more pressure on the server.
- Go for your shot and forget about the net player's poach. More shots are lost through errors by receivers who worry about whether the net player is poaching or not than through winners hit by net poachers. Focus on hitting your return as best you can.

Net Play in Doubles

- Volley to the open area or down the middle (see figure 4.14). This is the rule 99 percent of the time.
- Protect your alley when your partner is serving. Your job at the net is to protect your side first, then volley or smash any weak returns to the middle.
- Allow the player with the stronger smash to take the overhead down the middle.
- Aim volleys and smashes at the weaker opponent's feet. This increases the percentage of a weak return and may also "ice" the other team's better player by not allowing him or her to hit as often.
- Drop-volley when the opposition is behind the baseline.
- Poach some of the time. Fake the rest. You need to create the threat of a poach in the minds of the other team players. You can do this by poaching early in the match. Develop movements that appear to the receiver you are starting to poach, such as turning the head and body and taking a step across the middle (see figure 4.15). With a good fake, the result can be an easy put-away volley for the net player. Obviously, the better the server, the more often you can poach (and fake).

- Hit all out when poaching. The poach is a put-away shot that should be hit as hard as possible to the open area. You and your partner should decide what your plan will be after the poach, to continue to the other side of the court or retreat back to the same side.

- Learn your range of movement (as well as your partner's) as soon as possible (see figure 4.16). Teachers often advise teams to let the player with the stronger stroke take the ball down the middle. That is good advice as long as both players have equal ranges of motion and the ball comes exactly halfway between the two. This, of course, rarely happens. A more plausible solution is to have the players learn as quickly as possible which player has the greater range and to base the decision on which player's zone the ball comes into.

- Watch your opponents, not your partner, during play. To have the time to react to a ball, the net player must be looking at the opposition, not the partner.

- Adjust the net position as the situation demands. If you put enough pressure on the opposition by overwhelming them at the net, chances are they will adjust their strategy by lobbing more. If this happens, you should adjust your net position back from the net a few more feet so that the smash can be made easier. Against a team that seldom lobs, move up and tight to the net.

- When your partner's serve is weak, stand farther back from the net. You will be in a vulnerable position if the opposition attacks your partner's serve and comes to the net. To give yourself more time and a better position, move back closer to the service line if necessary.

Baseline Play in Doubles

- Place players on their stronger sides. The right-handed player with the better backhand should play the ad court.

- Use a crosscourt strategy when the opposition is up and back.

- When the opposition is up, hit down the middle. Shots down the middle lessen the angle of the return and may create confusion insofar as who should take the shot.

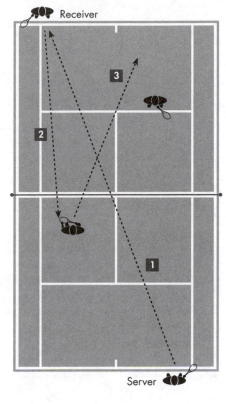

Figure 4.14

Volley to open area.

------> Path of Ball

Figure 4.15

Poach the return.

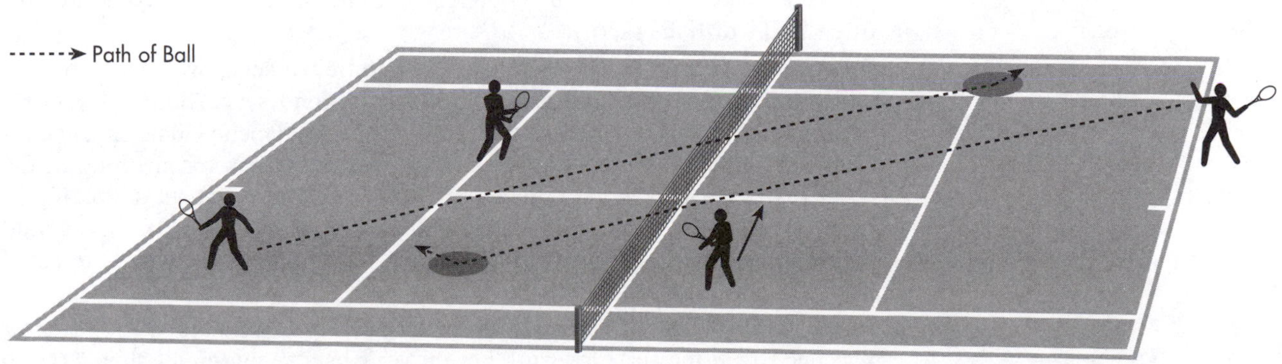

------> Path of Ball

Figure 4.16

Partner range of motion.

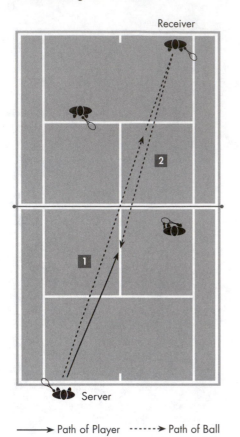

Receiver

2

1

Server

→ Path of Player   ┄┄► Path of Ball

■ Hit passing shots hard and low just over the net. Hard, low passing shots elicit weak, upward returns that can turn the advantage to your side.

■ Lob occasionally to keep the opposition off the net. A good team will move up on the net if you do not lob once in a while. Lobbing too much, however, may result in many easy points given up via the smash. Lob over the head of the player closest to you and move up to the service line. From there, a return lob can be smashed, or you can move up to the net to volley a weak groundstroke return.

■ Keep the net player honest by trying to pass occasionally. The key here is to hit the ball hard, keeping it well inside the alley.

■ When your partner is forced out of position, move to fill the hole. Players are taught to hit to the open areas. If you move to those areas, there is a better chance for a successful return (see figure 4.17).

■ Hit off-speed and low over the net once in a while. Interrupt the regular pattern of hard, low shots every so often to try and entice the opposition to overhit.

■ Approach on every opportunity. Good groundstrokes won't usually win the match. They can, however, give you opportunities, which must be taken advantage of, if the team is to be successful. For every weak return, hit a powerful approach shot and come in behind it. A high looping topspin forehand that lands deep is a good approach shot to follow to the net.

Anticipating Opponents' Strategies and Making Adjustments

Tennis players are always looking for an edge. Because so many variables are involved in the game of tennis, the ability to make adjustments during a match will profoundly influence your performance (and that of your opponent). No two players or teams are exactly alike. What strengths or weaknesses in your opponent are apparent? Your own game, too, will vary from day to day. On certain days, you may be stroking the ball particularly well and feel unbeatable. On other days, you may wish you'd taken up golf instead (golf might be a bad example). Regardless of the conditions, the following suggestions may help you anticipate your opponent's strategies and make the necessary adjustments to them:

■ Make your opponent play all the shots. Don't assume that your opponent can smash a lob effectively until he or she does so. You may have to sacrifice a few points to find out what your opponent's strengths and weaknesses are. It's often well worth the sacrifice.

■ Pressure the second serve. There is no telling how a server will react to what appears to be a receiver poised to attack the second serve. Some players remain unflappable, but others virtually fall apart. As Pancho Gonzalez once remarked, "Sometimes I could look across the court and see something in the other player's eyes that gave me a feeling he was worried about double-faulting. So I would maybe shade over a little bit to my forehand on his second serve, and a lot times he would double-fault. I got to the point where I felt as if I had the power almost to will the double fault."

■ Make adjustments in court position when playing big hitters. Stay a step or two deeper on the serve return. Shorten your backswing on all shots. Try to

Figure 4.17
Fill the gap.

time the return of serve rather than hitting it back with pace. Focus on keeping the opponent off the net by hitting the ball deep. Limit a powerfully executed shot to one point, not two or three. In other words, realize that some points will be won with power. Try as you will, you won't be able to stop the powerful shots completely. The important thing is not to let it cause you to lose the next point as well. With big hitters, your goal is damage control, not annihilation.

- Have patience when playing baseline players. These types of players can be extremely frustrating to play against, especially if their form is not as good as yours. Because they seemingly get everything back, each point must be fought for "tooth and nail." These players are often called "human backboards," for good reason. Accordingly, trying to beat baseline players at their own game is often an invitation to disaster. Use strategy to get them out of their game plan. Bring them to the net with low shots that lack pace. Attack the second serve and try to win the point at the net with well-angled volleys and smashes. Vary the pace of your shots. The baseliner relies heavily on getting his or her groundstrokes into the groove. Change angles, spins, placements, and pace constantly to keep the player off balance. Keep your cool. Just because you think you're the better player doesn't mean the match will be handed to you. You must prove it on the court.

- When playing younger players, keep the ball in play. Younger players traditionally have a more difficult time controlling their emotions. By keeping the ball in the court, frustration levels of younger players rise, which often causes them to beat themselves.

- When playing tall players, you may have to move up and time the service return. A tall player is able to hit the ball at a sharper angle because of the added margin of error over the net. By staying back on the return, that angle is increased, making the shot difficult to reach. Moving up is risky because you have less time to make a return, but at least you will be able to reach the ball.

- When playing left-handers, become a quick study. Right-handed players are used to attacking the weaker backhands of other right-handers. Unfortunately, this side is the forehand, the stronger side for a left-hander. In the heat of a match, old habits are often difficult to break. Many balls may be hit to the player's strength without thought. The left-handed player's shots also bounce and spin differently, making the job of returning the ball even more difficult. Use the first set to study how the ball travels and bounces. Expect the ball to spin to the opposite side after the bounce. Try to readjust your target to the opposite side for serves and other shots to the opponent.

Dealing with Weather and Other Environmental Conditions

Tennis is basically an outdoor sport, although its popularity has caused it to be moved indoors in some locations during the winter months. Adjusting to court surfaces and weather conditions are additional challenges to the tennis player. Most players can adjust fairly readily on their own to any environmental circumstance, but it is helpful to have a few guidelines that cover these situations.

- On fast courts (hard surfaces), the ball bounces lower and faster. Preparation time is thereby reduced. Players should adjust by standing deeper in the court and starting their racket preparation sooner.
- The advantage goes to the serve and volleyer on fast courts. Expect more forays into the net by servers. Take more chances yourself by going to the net.
- Slower courts such as clay favor the baseline player. Patience is important as is strategy. Matches usually last much longer, giving the advantage to the better-conditioned player.
- Don't rely on power as much on slow courts. Trying to hit aces may sap energy.
- Because slower courts take the power out of shots, players must generate their own power, using efficient stroke mechanics combined with vigorous effort.
- Good footwork is very important. A player with good court mobility will return many seemingly unreachable balls.
- On windy days, try and monitor changes in wind conditions as the match progresses. In general, play more aggressively when the wind is against you.
- When with the wind, keep shots low; when against it, hit higher and harder to keep the ball deep.
- Use a drop shot more when playing against the wind. The wind and underspin help carry the ball back toward the net after it has bounced.
- Play closer to the net when against the wind.
- When playing with a cross wind, hit high toward the alley and let the wind bring the ball back into the court. In this situation, opponents often let the ball go, thinking it will be out, only to find that the wind has blown the ball back into the court.
- In extreme heat, be wary of the dangers of heat exhaustion, dehydration, or muscle cramps. Watch carefully for signs of these problems and stop immediately if you encounter any of them.
- Hydrate yourself during each rest break. Even players accustomed to playing in hot weather should drink plenty of water during and after matches.
- Do not take salt tablets. Salt actually takes more water from the body's cells to dilute the concentration of sodium in the blood. Using salt tablets therefore dehydrates the body faster.
- Stay in the shade as much as possible between points and games.

- Wear loose-fitting, white clothing that reflects, not absorbs, the sun's rays.
- Wear a hat and use sunscreen.
- Try to keep your racket handle dry with a towel or wrist band.
- Keep the ball in play. Players wear out sooner in heat. Forcing the opponent to move as much as possible increases your chances of wearing the player down.

Learning by Watching

Have you ever really watched a tennis match? I mean *really* watched, not the way most spectators do. The average fan watches the ball during the rally and the players afterward. You know this is true because of the way the heads of the spectators move from side to side in unison with each shot. What you should be doing (if you want to learn through observation) is watching just the players during the rally.

Some tennis matches, because of the players involved, or the pressure, or both, are very entertaining and it's hard not to get caught up in the excitement. However, if your objective is to learn from watching good tennis players, then you should go about it somewhat systematically and resist the temptation to go with the flow. Here are a few suggestions on how to watch a match:

- If possible, try and watch a match live. Televised matches do offer some advantages such as slow motion replay and the commentator's analysis, but television does not give the viewer a realistic perspective as to the velocity or spin of the ball or the skills of the players.
- Try to separate the relevant technical elements of skill from the irrelevant ones. Many players have what some call idiosyncrasies, particular movements that may have some mental value to the player but that make no technical contribution to the skill. Boris Becker, for example, has a certain method of bouncing the ball as he rocks back and forth before the serve. Stefan Edberg performed a ritualistic footwork sequence just before his opponent began serving. Unsophisticated learners sometimes copy these idiosyncrasies, believing them to be important to skill performance. They should be recognized for what they are, simply trademarks of particular players that offer nothing to the performance of the skill.
- Watch the elements of stroke production. You should be able to pick out each of the elements of hitting a tennis ball such as the racket preparation, forward swing, and follow-through. When and how is the racket brought back? Where is the racket head on contact with the ball? Can you see the different methods of force such as angular and linear momentum being generated? Do the players use topspin or backspin? If so, notice the racket head positions before and after contact. Is the stance open or closed during groundstrokes?
- Watch the elements of the serve. How high is the toss? Notice the extension of the legs just prior to contact. Where is the contact point with the ball? What spin is put on the ball? Where is the ball served? What are the differences between the first and second serves?
- Watch the court movement. How do players move for balls both close and far away? Do they shade the court? How many steps do they take to reach the net after serving?
- How effective is the offensive game? Are players able to serve and volley? Why or why not? What sources of power are generated in the volley? Do they use much backswing? Can they execute the overhead smash effectively?
- Is there an effective defensive game? Do players lob enough? Too much?

- What elements of strategy are used? Are certain areas of the court being exploited? Does one player have a weakness that is being exploited by the other? Does each player rely on one type of shot to produce winners?
- In a doubles match, how do the teams line up to serve? Return serve? What is the strategy? Is one player hit to more than the other? What kinds of shots are used in doubles that are not used in singles? What adjustments do teams make in strategy during the match? Were they effective?

A good plan for watching matches is to bring a notepad with you and make notes as you see the movements performed on the court. List beforehand the different elements you will be looking for. Make only brief notations during the match and fill in the details afterward, otherwise you will forget much of what was observed.

Observational learning is a valuable method of mentally practicing tennis. Its value increases further when the information observed is incorporated into the skill repertoire and/or game plan. Although everything on the list may not be suitable, usually some elements can be imitated to the point where they can be useful additions.

Two other valuable forms of observational learning include getting a knowledgeable person to chart one of your matches, and having a teacher or coach give you an evaluation of your play. Charting involves tallying winners and errors and matching them with their respective shots (see table 4.1). It is essentially a record of how points were won and lost. Charting is a useful method of determining a player's strengths and weaknesses. Having someone give you qualitative feedback about your play can be a humbling experience but one that may provide several important insights into your game. Whatever observational learning methods are used, it is important not to try to incorporate everything learned into one's motor skill repertoire all at once. Focus on one thing at a time and be prepared for some plateaus in the learning curve.

TABLE 4.1 Shot Chart

Stroke	Winners	Errors
First serve		
Second serve		
Forehand serve return		
Backhand serve return		
Forehand groundstroke		
Backhand groundstroke		
Approach shot		
Forehand volley		
Backhand volley		
Half volley		
Drop volley		
Lob		
Smash		
Drop shot		

Glossary

ace A serve that lands in and beyond the reach of the opponent

ad court The left court

ad in The score when the server wins the next point after deuce

ad out The score when the receiver wins the next point after deuce

advantage The next point after deuce

alley A 4½ foot lane on both sides of the singles court used exclusively in doubles

angular momentum The force generated by the body's rotation

approach shot A shot immediately followed by an approach to the net

backcourt The area between the service line and the baseline

backhand groundstroke A stroke played on the backhand side of the body after the ball bounces

baseline The line farthest from and parallel to the net

baseline game A style of play in which the player hits mainly groundstrokes from the backcourt

baseliner A player who stays at or near the baseline during play and who rarely attempts to play in the forecourt

center mark The short line that divides the baseline at its center

closed face A downward angle of the racket face for hitting topspin

closed stance A body position where the feet are facing the sideline

continental grip The grip halfway between the eastern forehand and backhand that is used mainly for the volley

court The playing surface

crosscourt A shot in which the ball is hit diagonally from one side of the court to the opposite corner on the other side

deuce A tied game score of 40-40 as well as anytime thereafter when the score is even

double fault Failure to serve either the first or second ball into play

doubles A match between two teams of two players each

down-the-line shot A shot traveling parallel to the sideline

drop shot A shot hit lightly with backspin that barely clears the net

drop volley A soft shot played by the net player that just clears the net

eastern backhand The grip used for hitting backhand groundstrokes

eastern forehand The grip used for hitting forehand groundstrokes

elements In the context of tennis, the parts of a skill such as the backswing, forward swing, and follow-through of the forehand groundstroke

fartlek training A method of conditioning involving high-speed bursts of running followed by slow jogging

fault Failure to serve the ball into the proper service court

flat serve Also known as a cannonball, a serve hit hard with no spin

Flushing Meadows Home of the U.S. Open Tennis Championship in suburban New York City; played each autumn, the premier hardcourt tournament event of the ATP tour

foot fault An illegal serve caused by the server stepping into the court before contact of the racket is made with the ball

forehand groundstroke A stroke hit on the forehand side of the body after the ball bounces

game A part of a set consisting of a number of points. A player or team wins a game when four points are won and the side is ahead by at least two points. A game may also be won by the side who wins two consecutive points after 30-30 or deuce.

groundstroke A forehand or backhand stroke hit after the ball has bounced

gut A high-quality tennis string made from strips of twisted sheep gut

half-volley A shot hit immediately after the bounce

interval training A method of conditioning characterized by repeated periods of intense effort over a prescribed distance or time followed by active rest

let A replay of a point because of interference from a ball rolling onto the court or other causes

let serve A replayed serve; generally is a serve that hits the top of the net and lands within the proper service court

linear momentum The force generated by the transfer of body weight forward in the direction of the shot

lob A high, soft shot used to drive an opponent back to the baseline or allow the hitter more time to recover

love Zero in tennis scoring; may refer to no games or points won in a match

match A tennis contest involving either singles, doubles, or mixed doubles

match point A situation where the player ahead wins the match if he or she scores the next point

mixed doubles A match between two teams of one male and one female each

nap The fluff on a tennis ball

no ad A version of game scoring in which the first player or team to score four points wins the game

no-man's land The area between the baseline and the service line, so-called because it is a poor area to either attack from or defend

offensive lob An aggressive shot hit with high trajectory over the opponent's head and deep into the court

open stance A body position in which the front foot and upper body are facing the net

overhead A hard shot similar in motion to the serve that is usually hit from the front court

passing shot A ball hit low and hard to one side or the other of the player at the net

poach A movement to cut off the return of the receiver by a player at the net in doubles

progressive resistance exercise (PRE) A method of conditioning involving gradually increasing weights or other forms of resistance

pro set An abbreviated match that is complete when one player or team wins eight games and is ahead by at least two games

rally An exchange of shots back and forth across the net

ready position A stance in which the player awaits the ball with the feet shoulder-width apart, knees slightly bent, and racket held out in front of the body

receiver The player returning serve

second serve Following a service error, a second chance to serve the ball into play

serve and volleyer A player who serves and attacks the net attempting to win the point from the forecourt

service break Loss of a game by the server

service line A line parallel to and 21 feet from the net

set The part of a match consisting of a number of games. A player or team wins a set when six games are won and by a margin of at least two games.

singles A match between two players

skill-related fitness Those components of physical fitness such as agility, balance, coordination, reaction time, speed, and power that contribute to the performance of motor skills

skills In the context of tennis, the shots of the game such as serve, groundstroke, volley, overhead smash, and lob

slice A ball with underspin that is hit with an undercut motion

split sets A time during the match when each player has each won one or two sets

Stade Roland Garros Red clay courts in Paris, France, that are home each year to the French Open, where the best clay court players compete

straight sets Winning a match without losing a set

sweet spot The center of percussion and surrounding hitting zone of the racket face where the ball will be struck most effectively. In general, a 2- to 4-inch area in the middle of the racket face.

tennis elbow Technically known as radiohumeral bursitis; pain and inflammation of the elbow joint thought to be caused by a lack of follow-through when hitting the ball

tiebreaker A scoring system used when the set score reaches six games all. Although there are variations, a twelve-point tiebreaker is the most common. The first player or team to win seven points with at least a two-point advantage wins the tiebreaker and the set.

topspin Forward spin applied to the ball with an "up and over" motion of the racket

two-handed backhand A groundstroke played with two hands on the backhand side

USTA The United States Tennis Association; the governing body for organized tennis in the United States

volley A shot hit before the ball bounces

western forehand The racket is held with the hand positioned behind the handle so that the racket face is closed

Wimbledon Often called just The Championships, this major tournament draws the best players in the world and is played in early July on grass at the All England Club in Wimbledon, England

World Team Tennis An organization of the world's best professional tennis players

Index